24.1

The Case for Direct Democracy

Tony Adeney

•one®

• one publishing

Published under license to
•one publishing Sydney •one publishing New York
•one publishing London

First Edition 2004

British Library Cataloguing in
Publication Data available

ISBN 0-9542515-2-0

Typeset in Berling Roman
and Stone Sans.

ACKNOWLEDGMENTS

A special thanks to Mike Ker, Rob Clark,
Marc Smith, Hari Parmar, Ros Morley,
James McBride and Lorraine Roche.

Dedicated
to
Grace and George

A note from the author

Slowly and quietly it has gained support until it can now claim millions of followers around the world. From London to Bonn, New York to Tokyo, people are calling for its introduction. You might ask whether it's a new diet, a fantastic new pop band or a quasi-religious movement? I am pleased to say it is none of these. At first sight the answer seems mundane, but it has enormous implications for all of our lives. The future may be brighter than we thought. The future may not depend on politicians after all!

Tony Adeney

CONTENTS

SECTION ONE

-	Twenty Past Eight	1
-	Introduction	6
Chapter 1	What is Direct Democracy?	11

SECTION TWO

-	Horace Mop Head and the Green Gallstone	37
Chapter 2	A Beautiful Democracy	43
Chapter 3	Pulling the Strings of Power	66
Chapter 4	Monarchy & Parliament	79

SECTION THREE

-	Grumpy Dumpty	93
Chapter 5	The Missing Constitution	94
Chapter 6	The Rise of the Nation State	104
Chapter 7	Elizabeth II	113

SECTION FOUR

-	King Snear	123
Chapter 8	The European Union	130
Chapter 9	What Difference Does It Make?	143
Chapter 10	The EU and the Missing Millions	154

SECTION FIVE

-	Public Agent 0207	167
Chapter 11	Direct Democracy Discussion Forum	174
Chapter 12	Further Questions on Direct Democracy	206

SUMMARY

Chapter 13	Working Together	215
Glossary		217
Footnotes		223
Index		231

SECTION ONE

TWENTY PAST EIGHT

Britain no longer exists. OFFICIAL. Solomon's line manager, the salacious old git, had sent them all an email at twenty past eight that morning. Two seconds later, it was all over.

'Following regulation XT4891Y9 all territories formerly known as the United Kingdom of Great Britain and Northern Ireland will subsequently be referred to as Region 17. Amend relevant legislation - edit press releases and return to my desk by midday.'

Solomon always got the crap jobs and he knew it was because he wanted to be Jewish. Under a law passed in 2075, religious identities had been abolished together with a variety of other cultural misnomers. The intention had been to stamp out bigotry and racism but the Belgians had rioted, complaining about a loss of identity. After three months they had finally been subdued with a sop. A special decree had allowed them to watch all free-view programming earlier than other regions.

Solomon often talked to them on the interscan.

'Guess who will win Eurovision Fame Academy tonight?' they would tease.

'I am not interested in culture, I only watch the sports channel,' Solomon would reply irritably.

Solomon's work was mundane but he wasn't supposed to know the

1

bigger picture. Past, present and future legislation had to be amended. In time, he would become an unknown in the, 'magnificent construction of political brotherhood that countless years of struggle
had gifted the world.' So ran the opening paragraph in the government careers brochure. A political orphan at the age of ten, Solomon
lived in the shadow of failure. His father had been discovered editing
a subversive website and after the press had uncovered the scandal,
the shame had been too much.

Solomon could still picture his father falling silently past the grey
concrete panels, while he waited in the lobby for a lift home. At the
age of ten he'd been sent to a state orphanage. There they nourished
his interest in people management. The orphanage marked out
gifted children who showed an aptitude for organising their classmates, and Solomon had, as a result, won a series of scholarships.
Through school and university he had excelled. 'If you want to get
on, never say "yes" and never say "no," had been the lecturer's advice.
This lack of commitment had taken Solomon deep into the bowels of
government.

Solomon's appraisal had described him as quietly motivated and
capable of reaching a middle-management position. Sometimes, he
wondered what life must have been like before the polities had taken
control. Solomon's father had said that people used to vote for themselves, although apathy and corruption had put an end to that.
Nowadays, market research handpicked three polities who made all
the decisions. Government statistics had proven this to be demo-
graphically fairer and a more efficient use of resources.

Above Solomon's desk hung a buff-coloured poster. Stained with
nicotine, it read:

CURIOSITY IS HIGHLY ADDICTIVE
IT CAN LEAD TO A SLOW AND PAINFUL DEATH
Issued by the Department of Well Meaning.

Curiosity, as Solomon knew, was a heinous crime and punishable with re-education or death, but Solomon had a secret. Years ago, while reading Swallows and Amazons, he had become addicted to words. Lying under the sheets with a small chrome torch held tightly in his hand, he had cried the first time he read the book. Images had flooded into his blank mind and he knew his secret life had begun. Now his habit was out of control. Solomon would lie awake at night worrying that a word innocently spoken in his sleep might betray him.

Under the floorboards of his apartment, wrapped in oil-skins, Solomon kept bundles of illicit books: among them A. J. P Taylor's, History of the World; Albert Camus' The Outsider, Homer's Iliad and an Ikea catalogue. Although they had been difficult to find, Solomon would swap his clothing coupons for anything that contained words. Much of his collection was from private libraries that had escaped the purges of the fifties, after the owners had fled the country or been arrested.

Solomon knew the risks. He now had a collection of over two thousand words including a new one, 'Dorset', which he had heard recently on holiday. Sitting outside a pub, one of the locals had said it, not realising Solomon was nearby.

As a hushed silence had fallen, Solomon had spoken up,

'I won't report you, I collect words myself.'

The grizzled faces scowled at him. Not sensing the danger, Solomon had added,

3

'I only work for documentational support. I'm not an enforcer or anything like that.'

The men had turned away, saying nothing.

Just gone midday

Solomon's line manager picked at the dirt under his fingernails and lasciviously eyed Solomon through the two-way monitor. Solomon managed a thin smile: he recognised the face of bureaucracy incarnate.

His line manager's voice shrieked through the speaker,

'Solomon your project should have been completed by 12.30, I need you to work on a new project.'

Solomon peered at the screen, as a panel of statistics appeared.

It read:

1. **Over one hundred per cent of the population, are pleased to enjoy living standards.**

2. **More people than ever before have the benefit of continuous health monitoring.**

3. **The programme to re-educate miscreants is near its conclusion.**

4. **The guerrilla war near Babylon is now under control.**

This information meant nothing to Solomon. His skill lay in the fact that from these scant details he could write a forty-two page report, emphasising the benefits, making it sound highly credible but dull enough that nobody would read it.

Solomon murmured through the monitor's voice box,

'I'll stay in and work through my lunch.'

'You are my favourite now,' said the line manager leering.

Solomon winced.

The aroma of Cocoa, disinfectant and soya stew was rising from the basement. Sponsored by the Chemicox Corporation, tests had shown this to be the most conducive aroma for an efficient working environment. Chemicox supplied the dehydrated food packs, while staff only had to pay for the hot water. Solomon sat for a moment daydreaming. He was alone. Most of his colleagues were sitting outside, watching the sun above the darkly oiled river.

Solomon tentatively touched the keyboard and slowly typed D, dot, O, dot, R, dot, he hesitated, then looked around. There was nobody else in the office. He carried on typing S, dot, E, dot T. ENTER.

The screen fluttered then showed what seemed to be a tourist brochure with green and yellow images. It read, ' The picturesque region of Dorset offers fine views and sandy beaches. A favourite place for holidaymakers from all over the British Isles, Dorset remains an area full of local character, beauty and tradition.'

Solomon was transfixed and failed to hear the footsteps walk up behind him.

Oblivious to what was going on around him he was suddenly startled by a terse voice,

'Solomon B. Griswold, worker number 7694 HTY-47756-98573 - Sort code 7 - LOWER RANK. You are under arrest for the use and collection of illegal words. Please collect your belongings and come with us.'

As Solomon was led into the corridor his monitor flickered and it read:

OUR THOUGHT IS BETTER THOUGHT

PERCEPTION IS REALITY

THE SYSTEM WILL PROTECT YOU

Introduction

Imagine you lived in a country where you could propose laws, amend legislation, decide what your money was spent on and sack incompetent politicians. It sounds rather far-fetched but advances in technology mean that this is now possible in a way that it never was before. These days we can choose which pop star we watch on TV, we can vote on the Internet for our favourite film star, we can even select our favourite brand of coffee while shopping online. The same freedom to choose, can also be applied to democracy. It can cover issues as far wide ranging as taxation to child abuse - national parks to politicians' salaries - *but it gives you control over the decisions that affect your life.*

This type of democracy is called 'direct democracy' and has been used in various forms for over a hundred years. Switzerland is the only country where direct democracy is used extensively but it has proven to be popular in California, Denmark, Sweden, Norway and New Zealand. Popular that is with everybody except politicians, who fear losing their power and influence. At the same time, throughout the world people are becoming increasingly frustrated with politicians, who are failing on an unprecedented scale. Improvident bureaucracies, fraud and corruption have reduced people's trust in politicians to an all-time low. Most governments are dismissive of the electorate's wishes, but democracy was never intended to work this way. The ancient Greeks envisaged democracy as 'government of the people for the people,' not 'government of the people for the benefit of a few.' As Jean-Jacques Rousseau said, 'once democracy leaves the hands of the people, it ceases to be democracy in all but name'.

Bananas to you!

To explain how direct democracy works, I have used the UK (United Kingdom) as a model for our chosen system of direct democracy. However, the same principles could be applied to democracies from the United States to Japan, from France to Australia. *The idea is to demonstrate how direct democracy could work within any modern democracy.* Almost any democracy could be used as an illustration, but the UK is ideal for a variety of reasons. It has the longest established 'popular democracy' in the world, its representative form of government has been a model for many other countries and Westminster's Parliament is widely regarded as an efficient and popular means of government. This view is one that has been romanticised, as the reality is that the British public have shown a growing dissatisfaction with their politicians. During the general election of 2001, 41 per cent of the British electorate failed to vote; many feeling that there were no parties worth supporting.[1] In 2002, during the local county elections, 65 per cent of the electorate didn't vote![2]

In Hartlepool in 2002, local people were so disenchanted with the major political parties that they elected as mayor a man dressed in a monkey suit, after he campaigned for 'free bananas for children'![3] Peter Mandelson, a former government cabinet minister, was one of the bemused audience who watched as the monkey was elected mayor by over 60 per cent of those who voted. The evening turned into farce when a Downing Street official commented that,

'It is only expected that new faces come to the fore.'[4] Electing a man in a monkey suit is certainly entertaining but the people of Hartlepool were making a very serious protest. They had lost confidence in the major political parties' ability to represent them.

Trust me I'm a politician

In 2003 a study of the British electorate showed that only 16 per cent of the public, 'were prepared to trust the government most, or all, of the time'.[5] So why have the public become so disillusioned? The size, power and influence of the British government have seen enormous growth in the last forty years, with seemingly less benefit for its citizens. In 1904 the British government was spending 13 per cent of the UK's Gross National Product (GNP). At the same time the UK was a highly successful industrial nation leading the world in terms of innovation, services and industrial capacity. By 1994 government spending had risen to 45.5 per cent of the UK's gross domestic (GDP), yet there has been a relative decline in the quality of many publicly run services compared to other modern nations.[6]

By 2005 the British government is expected to spend around £350 billion of taxpayers' money. Such a huge sum ought to give the UK some of the best public services in the world, but there is a widening gap between what the public expect and what they get. With rhetoric being used as a substitute for effective management, and government figures presented to put a positive spin on poor results, there is growing cynicism. The public see that every issue, from crime to litter, or immigration to transport, is more likely to receive the attention of a committee writing reports than anyone taking effective action.

Unfortunately, this problem is not common to the UK alone. In most countries there has been a tendency for the bureaucracy of government to grow at great cost, without anyone being account-able to the electorate. So what is happening? In the UK, as in most democracies, every five years the public vote for someone to repre-sent them. These elected representatives in the United Kingdom are known as Members of Parliament, or MPs, who work in the House of Commons at Westminster, with the Prime Minister its most senior figure. In the United States the House of Representatives and the Senate take a similar role, with the execu-tive headed up by the President. In other countries the systems vary but are essentially the same.

As the electorate vote for politicians to make decisions on their behalf, this is referred to as 'representative democracy'. What we have seen is a tendency for these representatives to pay less and less attention to the needs of voters, until an election is imminent. At that point voters are promised that everything will improve if people just vote for them one more time. Although this is known as 'representative democracy', in reality, it is far from representative.

24.1% of voters

In the British General Election of 2001, of 44.7 million people who were eligible to vote, only 10.8 million people voted for New Labour who won the election.[7] *This means that only 24.1 per cent of the British electorate voted for a political party that gained 86 per cent of the parliamentary seats.*[8] In other countries these anomalies are even more absurd. In 2001 George. W. Bush was elected President of the United States of America even though he received 539,898 less votes than his main rival Al Gore![9]

The problem is that election results increasingly depend on marginal constituencies, so government policies have less and less relevance to the wishes of the majority. In the UK only 3 per cent of the electorate now holds sway over who will form a government.[10]

Consequently, the major political parties address their policies towards a small but highly influential group of voters in marginal constituencies.

Representative democracy has a far more profound failing. Voting for one political party cannot represent your views, because you are only offered a package of policies. *Much of which you might disagree with.* This all-or-nothing package is based on a manifesto that the electorate have no control over. You might choose to vote for a party that promises more investment in health, and as a result the armed forces are cut back? Or you might choose to vote for a party promising to be tougher on crime and as a consequence public transport is privatised. Voting for a political party is not an accurate way of assessing your needs.

Moreover, with increasingly lucrative salaries and expenses packages, politics has attracted more and more 'career politicians' with little experience outside of politics. More value is now placed on what someone says, than what someone has achieved. The fact that a politician makes 'an eloquent speech,' or 'is a good speaker,' may help them to score political points but doesn't do much else. Add to this the way that governments are now influenced by secretive lobbying and political deals and you begin to realise why so many democracies are failing. Even newly elected politicians soon realise that they have little influence over decisions that are made.

Representative democracy has evolved to augment the personal interests and ambitions of a small political elite, not the public it is supposed to be representing. Fortunately, there is an alternative.

Chapter One

What is Direct Democracy?

Direct democracy allows the electorate to vote directly on questions of policy, to propose legislation, to remove errant MPs and to veto unnecessary or unwanted laws. You only need look to Switzerland to see how effective it can be. Switzerland has one of the most stable, affluent and environmentally sustainable economies in the world. The electorate have the right to vote on issues ranging from taxation to transport, or the environment to criminal sentencing. The distrust of politicians that exists in many other countries is not to be found there. Switzerland is a relatively small country, but *it is important to realise that advances in technology, has made direct democracy possible for any size of nation*. So what would you like to see? More hospitals, better public transport, less roads, more roads, lower taxes, higher taxes?

Few of us have ever been asked such questions before, but we are still expected to pay our taxes, uphold the law and go quietly about our business. In return we are given little influence over the decisions that affect our lives. A handful of politicians propose policy and even less of them make the real decisions. This can hardly be described as democratic.

We know that politicians are good at being elected but why should this qualify them to run a country? Nowadays, politicians manage huge budgets that cover areas in which they have little expertise. These same ministers are frequently moved from one department to another before they have had time to get to grips with the issues, while government officials and the public are left to deal with the consequences. A continual drive to 'make one's mark' on education, health, trade, crime and transport produces a stream of regulations and targets, which is not only highly inefficient, it is thoroughly demoralising and expensive for the taxpayer.

Accountability and democracy

Direct democracy forces politicians to be more accountable in a variety of ways. For instance, the public would have the right to vote on politicians' salaries and pension rights, if proposed increases were above the rate of inflation. In 1996, to the dismay of many, British MPs voted themselves a salary increase of 25 per cent.[1] This huge increase was made by the same MPs who'd been complaining that company bosses were paying themselves too much! At the same time most of the public received a pay rise in the region of 1 per cent. In 1997 the Chancellor of the Exchequer Gordon Brown abolished the dividend tax credit, which cost people with private pensions £5 billion. This had to be made up with higher contributions from both employees and employers.[2]

At the same time, British MPs voted themselves a pension rise equivalent to a 38 per cent increase in benefits.[3] W.M. Mercer, an international actuary company, calculated that if an MP were to keep his parliamentary seat for twenty years he would accumulate pension entitlements of £630,000.[4] These same MPs only have to work up until the age of sixty to receive a full pension, while the public have to work until they are sixty-five, or in many cases longer.[5] In 2003 the Lord Chancellor Lord Irvine received a 'pension bonus' of £2 million, on top of his annual salary of £202,736, and this did not include expenses or pension entitlements accrued in previous positions. The leader of the government opposition party described the award as 'outrageous'.[6]

Direct democracy could also be applied to other areas of government, for instance politicians might be encouraged to work on placements to gain practical experience and local people could be consulted over the placements in their area. By shortening their holidays (MPs are only required to attend Parliament for an average of 24 weeks a year[7]), MPs would be placed in such sectors as hospitals, schools, nurseries and prisons, enabling them to gain a better understanding of public services. It would give politicians an opportunity to help their constituents in a direct and practical way, while appreciating the issues that many people experience on a daily basis.

Stakeholders in prosperity

The UK is a wealthy country; it has the fourth largest economy in the world.[8] Yet, while government spending increases, the quality of life for many people deteriorates. The British public now have to work until 2 June every year just to pay their taxes. At the same time, if hidden taxes such as VAT are taken into account, taxes have risen dramatically in recent years. Many costs such as the Community Charge (similar to a local property tax) lie outside the government's definition of taxation, but in reality it is just another tax. In 1900 there existed around 50,000 government civil servants, today there are in the region of 650,000[9] (and these figures do not include all of the 'extra government bodies', where there is little accountability or transparency over how your money is spent).

Although overt corruption in British government is relatively uncommon, many departments have grown into huge bureaucratic monoliths. For example, the total education budget for England is

£41,984 million.[10] Of this, £11,515 million is spent by the Department for Education and Skills (DfES) and Local Education Authorities (LEAs). Only a fraction of the money intended for education is spent on pupils.[11] What seems to be true is that 'those who can teach, teach, those who can't go about writing long-winded management efficiency schemes!' More taxpayers' money is wasted by a second tier of government, known as the European Union (EU), to which the UK now contributes around £20 billion a year.[12] British people work the longest hours in Europe and take the shortest holidays, while subsidising other European countries that have a better quality of life and cheaper living costs.[13] Yet, the British public have never been consulted over whether they want to continue with this arrangement.

The public's frustration with the EU was evident when, in June 1999, 76 per cent of the electorate declined to vote in the European Elections, despite an extensive government campaign encouraging the public to support the elections.[14] The problem is that with increasing bureaucracy, a lack of accountability and a distancing of politicians from the needs of the electorate, the general public have lost confidence in their leaders. The UK has an incredible legacy of art, language, literature, theatre, scientific research, engineering, technology, architecture, music, sport and comedy. From Isaac Newton to the Beatles - from Shakespeare to James Bond, the UK has excelled in almost every area, yet the public seem to have lost confidence in themselves.

Referendum and proposals

So how is direct democracy different? Basically, with direct democracy the public have the right to take part in the decision-making process. Voters are allowed to propose, amend, review and veto laws, legislation and taxes with the use of referendum and consultation. *Legislation would still be passed by government but issues that are important to the public would be decided by the public.* For instance, if there was a controversial piece of government legislation, it could be forced to a public referendum. A referendum would require 2 per cent of the electorate to sign a petition (at either national or local level) within 180 days. This would then allow for the matter to be put to voters in a referendum.

The final decision would only take effect if over 50 per cent of the eligible electorate voted to support the initiative (defined as 50 per cent of the eligible electorate plus one). To gain a petition with support from 2 per cent of the electorate is quite a hurdle, so it means that only questions that are important to voters would be decided by referendum. The majority of laws would still have to be passed by government but the electorate would have the final say. The outcomes of these referendums would be binding, although a process of scrutiny could be factored in.

There are many recent examples of how direct democracy has been put into practice.

- In California, in October 2003, a local politician was removed from office following a popular referendum.

- In Switzerland, in 2003, following a popular initiative and a national referendum, a woman - whose daughter was violently raped and left for dead - succeeded in changing the law on the sentencing of violent criminals and paedophiles[15]

- In 2001 the Danish people voted not to adopt the new European currency, the Euro.

- In 2001 New Zealanders blocked a law that was intended to ban alcohol advertising.

- In April 1997 in the United States, the Californians voted to reduce property taxes.

- In 1997 New Zealanders voted against the details of a government pension scheme, with 91.8 per cent of the electorate voting against it.

- A new constitution was approved by the Spanish people in a referendum on 6 December 1978.

- In 1981 the Italians voted in a referendum to amend their abortion laws.

- In 1997 both Scotland and Wales voted for devolution.

- In 2005 the city of Edinburgh is planning to have a referendum asking local people if they would like to see a congestion charge applied to the inner city area.[16]

Referendums are not limited to questions of national interest alone. In the small alpine town of Glarus in Switzerland the local people voted to build a new traffic roundabout on the Southern side of their town. The right to vote on government legislation is written into the Swiss constitution.[17]

Many people in the UK are unaware that people in parish councils in England already have the right to call a referendum on local issues. Under a law passed in 1972, which applies to English parishes (but not cities!) and small communities in Wales, a referendum can be called if ten or more people attending a parish council demand it. Although this facility has been used on a variety of occasions it has received little publicity:

- In 1998 during a fire-fighters' dispute in Essex, a popular referendum was called asking local people if they wanted to cut fire-fighting services.

- In the year 2000, trials for genetically modified crops were abandoned in St Osyth after local community raised a petition and gave their support to a referendum.

- Councils in Devon, Cornwall, Dorset, Lincolnshire and Wiltshire consulted local people over whether they wanted to keep the British pound rather than introduce the Euro currency. The response was clear: 93.8 per cent said that they wanted to keep the British pound.

- The village of Shoreham, near Sevenoaks in Kent, voted over whether a disgraced First World War soldier should be included on a local war memorial.

- The city of Bristol in the South West of England called a referendum to decide on how much Community Charge should be levied.

- Soon after this, the London borough of Croydon did the same [18]

Despite its popularity, the public are rarely offered the chance to express their views. On the rare occasions that the British government has called a national referendum, it has spent large amounts of the taxpayers' money telling people how they should vote.

So how does direct democracy work?

Direct democracy can be applied to all levels of government administration, from central government to regional and local councils. Referendums are just one important aspect of direct democracy and could be triggered in a variety of ways. The most important of these is the popular initiative. A new piece of legislation or a change in the law could be proposed by anyone eligible to vote. Proposals could be made at either national or local level, would have to be seconded by twelve names, and would have to be confirmed by a legal affidavit. The proposer would then have 180 days to gain a minimum of 2 per cent of the relevant electorate's support.

Once the required number of signatures had been collected the proposal could be entered into a referendum. At this stage it would remain a proposal. *It wouldn't become legislation until the majority of the electorate had voted for it.* Then, once the referendum takes place, the electorate would be asked if they wanted the proposal to become law. This would require that over 50 per cent of the electorate voted in favour of the proposal, which means only proposals voters felt strongly enough about would become legislation. It would not be possible to bring forward a proposal that contradicted constitutional rights, as defined in a written constitution.

In a referendum you would be able to vote 'for', 'against', or 'not sure' (in other words abstain) or you could choose not to vote at all. Voting would not be compulsory. For a proposal to become a law, more than 50 per cent or more of the total amount of registered voters would need to vote 'yes'.

If someone did not vote, it would be assumed that they did not want the proposal to become law. *Regardless of whether or not you vote, you are still taken into account.* This avoids the problem of small numbers of activists, forcing through legislation that the majority of people do not want. The present electoral system only takes into account those who vote.

Parliamentary initiatives

A simple majority in the House of Commons would force a parliamentary initiative on any piece of government legislation. The proposal would then be passed to a national referendum, where the electorate would make the final decision. The same system would apply to local government, where people could vote on such issues such as Community Charge increases.

Popular veto

If 2 per cent of the electorate signed a petition - within a period of 180 days - against a current piece of legislation that the government was attempting to make law, the legislation would be suspended until a referendum could take place. This would enable the electorate to veto unnecessary or unwanted legislation. Then if more than 50 per cent of the electorate voted to veto the legislation it would be withdrawn.

If the required amount of votes was not reached it would proceed as before. A popular veto could only take place while the law was being passed through Parliament, not once it had become law. Once a popular veto had been initiated, the government would have a statutory duty to wait 180 days to see if the petition could raise enough support.

Personnel Recall initiatives:

The electorate vote for MPs or councillors to represent them, so voters should have the right to remove them. This happened in California in October 2003, when Governor Gray Davis was removed with a popular initiative that gained 1.2 million supporters. Eventually, actor Arnold Schwarzenegger was elected to replace him. In our system of direct democracy MPs could be removed in the same way. If this were to occur, severance pay would be limited to two months' pay and pensions contributions would be terminated at that point.

A popular recall could only be triggered by a petition of 10 per cent of the relevant electorate (the figure is high to avoid the system being abused) within a constituency over a period of 180 days.

It could not be applied to senior cabinet ministers or the Prime Minister. The decision would then go to a referendum either at local or national level. The MP or councillor wouldn't be suspended or removed until a majority, of more than 50 per cent of the electorate had voted to do so. The referendum would have to take place within three months of completing the petition and this would necessitate a by-election to vote for a replacement MP. This measure could be limited to cases of serious misconduct or incompetence such as fraud and corruption.

Of course, some politicians are quick to raise objections to direct democracy but we should determine whether or not their objections are justified. Below are some common myths, questions and answers relating to direct democracy.

The electorate are not sophisticated enough to understand certain issues.
The implication here is that politicians have superior intellects. Today most people are educated, literate and more than capable of understanding the issues that affect their lives. Indeed, the majority of the electorate have more 'commonsense' than they are given credit for. Many ordinary people have a better understanding of what needs to be done, as, unlike politicians, they use the public services every day.

So it's not just politicians that could propose legislation?
Correct, with direct democracy anyone who has the right to vote has the right to make a proposal. If enough names are collected within the time allowed, the proposal is put to the electorate in a referendum. Particular age groups could even vote on specific issues. For instance, teenagers could have the right to vote on certain decisions that only affect them.

How would voting in a referendum work?

At present when an election is held, the government hires out polling stations, staff and adjudicators. Then millions of pieces of paper are counted by hand. This is inefficient and expensive. With today's technology there's no reason why voters can't be issued with an electronic card that holds their voting rights, driving licence, insurance details and could be used as an identity card (If we wanted one). It could be similar to a bank card with a PIN number, signature and photograph.

Machines like cash dispensers or ATMs could be placed in town halls, libraries, schools or supermarkets. Voters would simply put in their card and register their vote. Voting could take place over a period of a week and once collected, the information would be sent directly to a central computer. The results would only be announced once all the votes had been collected.

Does the technology exist to make this work?

Yes, it is relatively straightforward. Many countries have national lottery schemes that use thousands of machines to collect data from all over the country. This system of collecting data has proven to be accurate, fast and reliable. At a later stage there would be the possibility of telephone, internet, email and television voting but to start with 'electronic voting' machines could be situated in public locations. Switzerland is way ahead and is now in the process of introducing the e-vote, which allows people to vote from their home computers. This will make voting easier for many people who find it difficult to vote, such as the disabled, the elderly or those who are just too busy.[19]

Surely many countries are too large to be run this way?

Not any more! What is amazing is that new technology makes

direct democracy practical for any size of nation, whatever its population or geographic makeup.

Would people understand what to do?

Staff would be available to advise on how to use the equipment. A final list of the questions that would appear in the referendum would be published six weeks before voting was due to take place. This would give people enough time to consider the proposals and whether or not they wanted to vote. Voters would also be allowed to choose which questions to vote for.

Would everyone have to vote?

No. A referendum vote would only be binding if the proposal were agreed on by over 50 per cent of the eligible electorate (defined as 50 per cent plus one vote). *As things stand today, your views are not taken into account if you don't vote.* With our model of direct democracy, if you don't vote it would be assumed that you do not want the proposal to become law. This would minimise the problem of introducing legislation that the majority of the electorate don't want. In the London mayoral election, the winner, Ken Livingstone, only received 667,877 votes as a first choice candidate, from 5.5 million eligible voters. This is equivalent to 12 per cent of the eligible vote. Voters were not given the option to vote against the introduction of a mayor for London.[20]

Why are there different options when voting?

A 'yes' vote means that you would like to see the legislation in place. You can vote 'no' if you feel the legislation would be wrong. You can tick 'not sure' (the equivalent of abstain) if you are unsure of the proposal. You can also choose not to vote. The options enable others to gauge public opinion about a proposal. It might be that people want change but not in a way that has been proposed, so they might tick 'not sure'.

If there were a large amount of 'not sures' or abstentions it would encourage the original proposer to amend the proposal and attempt to introduce the legislation at a later date. If the initiative did not reach the 50 per cent plus one votes required it would be rejected. The same initiative could not be put forward again for two years. It would not be possible to carry over petitions to another referendum and only one question would be allowed on each petition. Government would not be allowed to introduce the same legislation for a period of two years.

Would we have to vote for everything?
No, only issues that the electorate felt strongly about. Proposals would only be put to the electorate if there were enough support for them. *Most legislation would still be handled by government.* At the same time, direct democracy would force the government to be more considerate of the electorate's wishes.

Don't we need politicians to make the tough decisions?
What we see time and time again is that politicians don't make the tough decisions. For example, in March 2004, the government approved the introduction of genetically modified crops even though an independent poll of the British public showed that over 90 per cent of the public did not want them.[21]

Would we have to vote every week?
No, voting would take place once or twice a year. Raising enough names for a petition would take time and effort. Proposers would only attempt a petition if they thought it likely they would get enough public support and any petition would have to be com-

pleted within 180 days of the original application. The number of proposals would be limited to forty at any given referendum, and if there were more than forty petitions, the proposals with the most signatures would go forward (although this could be amended if there was enough support for it).

Wouldn't we get some crazy laws?

This is unlikely, why would the electorate vote for poor legislation that they had to live with? The hurdle of collecting enough signatures would filter out most of these problems. To propose something via a referendum could take over a million signatures. Most people have better things to do with their time.

What about the possibility of fraud?

A voting card with a signature, photograph and PIN number would reduce the amount of fraud that takes place in today's system. At present it is difficult to verify a person's identity and there are examples of people voting more than once.

Wouldn't it take too long to get legislation passed?

The process is not fast but at the moment legislation can take years to pass into law. It is also important that the electorate has enough time to consider any proposals. At present the larger political parties dominate the legislation that is put forward and they always give priority to their own policies. Laws are rarely passed on merit; they are passed on whether or not they have enough government backing. Often good legislation has been deliberately rejected or 'talked out' rather than the government lose credibility. This legislation still has to checked and amended by lawyers with all the costs incurred, even when the government has no intention of allowing it to become law.

Would these referendum decisions be binding?

Yes. There is little point in asking the electorate to express their wishes only to ignore them. A person elected as 'People's Chancellor' could oversee any referendum proposals into becoming law and would be responsible for checking that referendums were carried out fairly. The People's Chancellor would be chosen by the electorate and no one who had been a member of a political party in the last ten years would be allowed as a potential candidate.

A process of scrutiny by the House of Lords, or as in the United States by the House of Congress, could also be built in. If the second house had a fundamental objection to the proposal, the proposal could be held over for 180 days. (These objections would have to be convincing enough to challenge the wishes of the electorate). During this period the 'opposer' could attempt to gain enough signatures (again 2 per cent) to cancel the legislation at the next referendum. *If the opposer did not gain the 50 per cent plus one vote support, the original proposal would become law.*

How would popular vetoes work?

If a referendum confirmed that the electorate had rejected a piece of government legislation, that legislation would be dropped. The same or a substantially similar piece of legislation could not be proposed again for a period of two years from the date of a referendum decision. The People's Chancellor would be an autonomous judicial figure, independent of any political party.

Would the electorate have the right to call a referendum on any subject?

This wouldn't be practical. The public would have the right to call a referendum on most subjects, but with some exceptions.

For example, issues over National Security and Defence would still have to be decided upon by government, but almost every other aspect of government could be scrutinised by the electorate. We can look to the Swiss system as an example of what subjects might be excluded in national referendums.

What is meant by a written constitution?
Most countries have a written constitution. The UK differs in that it has a constitution based on precedent, contained within acts of Parliament and the government's prerogative (the right to make decisions without consulting Parliament or the electorate). A written constitution would be integral to safeguard people's rights, so that no proposals could be agreed, that contradicted British citizen's right as regards principles of free speech, religion, race, gender, sexuality or disability.

We don't have a tradition of referendum!
This excuse is often used to discourage nations from adopting direct democracy, but how can we have a tradition of something that has not been available? Countries didn't have a tradition of women voting, until women campaigned for the right to do so.

What about the rights of women?
With the whole electorate able to vote on decisions, women would have a proportionally greater influence than they have now because they could express their wishes on specific issues, as opposed to relying on elected representatives who are predominately men. At the present time in the British Parliament, of 659 MPs only 119 are women.[22] At the same time most of the secretarial, administrative, catering and cleaning staff at Westminster are women!

Wouldn't some people feel left out?

In Switzerland, their system of direct democracy was introduced because there are so many diverse cultural groups. Switzerland has four national languages and a variety of ethnic groups[23] In many countries the majority of the electorate feel left out because they have so little influence over decisions that are made.

Would it mean that the majority of the electorate would always have the final say?

Government votes on a majority basis, we vote at elections on a majority basis. Why shouldn't the electorate be able to vote on all issues on a majority basis? Direct democracy is fairer than any other system of democracy because everyone has an equal vote and is entitled to persuade others of their argument. The rights of minority groups and small communities would be protected within a written constitution.

What about minority groups?

I believe that minority groups want much the same as everyone else: less crime, more opportunity and a better standard of living. In recent years in Southern France and Austria, there has been a dramatic rise in the support of extreme right-wing political parties, primarily because their governments have ignored the concerns of most of their voters.

Could the government attempt to unfairly influence the electorate before a vote?

It would be made illegal for any government to spend taxpayers' money campaigning on questions to be decided in a referendum. At the present time, politicians are allowed to spend taxpayers' money campaigning for government policies. In the UK, the government now spends more on advertising than any other single organisation. Two weeks before a referendum it would be illegal for campaigning to continue, whether by politicians, the media, private companies or individuals. In many countries such a law already exists during voting periods.

How would initiative questions be phrased?
Any referendum proposal would contain a summary of the question and detail what the legislation entailed. The final legislation would have to accurately reflect the original proposal. The People's Chancellor would be responsible for seeing this through. Past referendums in Switzerland, California and Denmark give some insight into how questions might be phrased.

Wouldn't the country descend into chaos?
The government would still be in control but it would be *more accountable to the people they are representing*. At the present time, many countries experience extreme change every time a new government is elected. Direct democracy enhances stability and reduces the need for political u-turns.

Wouldn't direct democracy undermine the economy?
Switzerland uses direct democracy and is one of the most stable and affluent countries in the world. So does California, which has one of the highest standards of living in the world. Without unnecessary interference from government their people and industries have flourished while retaining a diverse cultural identity.

Who pays for the laws that are introduced?
All proposals entered into a referendum would have to be costed and made clear in the referendum proposal. The people of Switzerland even have control over what money the government can spend. The government is allocated a yearly budget and the

government has to work within that budget. We would introduce the same measures to the UK within our model.

You might think that the Swiss would vote for lower taxes and free beer for everyone but they don't. Many pieces of popular legislation are passed that save money and reduce government bureaucracy. In 1998 the Swiss voted to raise the tax on petrol, and in 1997 they voted to abolish a government department that was shown to be wasting money![24]

Wouldn't pressure groups try to affect decisions?

It is far more difficult to buy the influence of the whole population than a handful of politicians. As you will see, politicians are not adverse to being influenced themselves. The amount of money spent by large corporations lobbying politicians in America, Europe and Asia is staggering. In Brussels, at the heart of the European Government, political lobbying has become a multi-billion Euro industry.

Why would government be more accountable?

At the moment, rather than controlling spending or dealing with inefficiencies, governments tend to increase taxes or simply borrow more money. With direct democracy the public would also have access to accounts, showing how their money is spent. Each year the government would have a duty to publish the percentage of GNP spent by any government and how much it had borrowed that year.

No taxes could be raised above the rate of inflation unless the electorate agreed. In the long term, democracies would be aiming for less government not more. In the UK, the same principle could be applied to income tax, VAT, and Community Charge. In 2002 many British people saw their Community Charge bill rise by as much as 20 cent, with little justification and no recourse to the law.

In our system of direct democracy, tax rises would be limited to the rate of inflation, unless the electorate voted otherwise. In California in 1978, a measure proposed by Howard Jarvis and Paul Gann managed to cap property taxes at 1 per cent after a popular referendum received the support of 65 per cent of local people, despite government opposition.[25]

Would voting be affected by the latest media headlines?

The process of petitioning a proposal could take up to a year. It is important to be able to debate issues in the media and there would be plenty of time to do this. People working in the media have a wide range of views, which is healthy in a democratic society. The same argument could be used during general elections or during any other debate. Two weeks before any referendum, campaigning on issues contained within the referendum would be banned.

How would direct democracy be an improvement?

At the moment, people vote for one party and one manifesto. They either accept everything or nothing. *With direct democracy people only vote for policies that they want.* Politicians would find it more difficult to introduce legislation that the majority of people did not want. Politicians would be more careful about the decisions they make, if they knew the electorate had the power to remove them!

If this system is so good why it being used now?

Direct democracy hasn't been introduced because politicians are unlikely to give up power voluntarily.

Wouldn't the larger political parties still have more influence?

A limit would be put on the amount of money that could be spent by any one political party at an election or referendum.

For instance, it might be limited to £10 million (increasing yearly with the rate of inflation) in the UK or $100 million in the United States. In the last British election in 2001, the two main parties spent around £38 million, far more than all other political groups together.

In the United States it has been estimated that the two largest political parties spent in the region of $1 billion in the period before the election.[26] This type of campaigning only distorts the democratic process because whoever spends the most money has the most influence.

Would direct democracy put a halt to the rise of politicians who are only interested in their own careers?

Possibly. Political candidates would be asked to publish a profile of their work experience, and a minimum age of thirty would be set for entering government. This would allow candidates to gain experience outside the world of politics. The proportion of MPs who have had careers other than 'gilded political career paths,' such as researchers, barristers or journalists has fallen from 80 per cent in 1951 to 31 per cent in 1997.[27] Apparently, in the 1992 intake of MPs there were several who even approached the whips office to ask when they would be made ministers![28]

Would there still be a role for the government?

Yes, but a more limited one. We would still need governments to legislate but voters would have more control over any decisions that are taken. The role of the government would still be important but they would become servants of the people, rather than masters.

Would we still need a prime minister or president?

Yes, and they would be chosen from the majority party. As direct democracy develops political parties will be less important than the opinion of the electorate. Why should political parties have such a monopoly on power, especially when they are so influenced by those who fund them?

Would it be an infringement on people's liberties if the government knew which way they had voted?

At present, when you vote at elections there is a registration number on the voting paper, which means the government already has a record of who voted and what for. Voting for a series of questions would be no different.

Would we not get politicians campaigning on single issues?

Possibly, but voters would still want to know their views across a range of subjects. In Switzerland, there have been various single-issue parties but they have tended to do badly in elections. Voters still want to see a balanced set of policies from candidates. Campaigning on a single issue rarely answers the electorate's concerns.

Will there still be a role for the monarch?

Although the UK is unusual in still having a constitutional monarch, the Head of State acts as a final check on the abuse of power by the executive government. In the last sixty years, on three occasions the UK's monarch has directed Parliament when a working government has not been possible. The monarch offers stability and coherence to British democracy.

Would there still be a role for a second chamber?

Yes, they would still have an important part to play in Parliament but it would become more representative of society. New Labour originally proposed a completely elected second chamber, but they now seem to want to appoint their own members to the House of Lords! How this is more democratic than hereditary peers is a mystery! Eventually, all members of a second house would be elected by the public for a set term of five years. This would be open to all responsible citizens. Members in the second chamber who had previously worked as MPs would be limited to 20 per cent. In the UK, at the present time, 167 members of the Lords were originally MPs.[29]

Do people want direct democracy?

In 1995 the Joseph Rowntree Trust commissioned Mori to conduct a poll asking people in the UK if they would prefer direct democracy to the present 'representative' system of government. The result was that 77 per cent said that they would prefer direct democracy.[30] In other countries similar polls have reflected the same feeling: in the United States 76 per cent of the public were in favour; in Germany 71 per cent; in France 66 per cent and in Belgium 51 per cent.[31]

If people voted for direct democracy could the present politicians stop it?

No, if enough of the population voted for direct democracy it would be introduced.

How could a system of direct democracy be put in place?

The only effective way of introducing direct democracy would be to allow people to vote for it. There are many groups around the world campaigning for direct democracy, including Direct Democracy International, which brings together key figures from these different organisations. The beauty of direct democracy is that these organisations are led by the needs of the electorate not an overriding political dogma. Ultimately, it is for the electorate of countries themselves to decide if they would like to see direct democracy introduced and what policies they would like to support. Direct Democracy International works with local people to give advice on supporting candidates in elections and campaigning. More information can be found on the Direct Democracy International website at:

www.directdemocracyinternational.com

Once in place, would we still need direct democracy candidates?
Not necessarily, the most important thing is to set up a fair and equitable system of democracy, encompassing the rights of all citizens. Once in place, which political party you support would be less important, as you would have more influence on government decisions.

When could direct democracy be introduced?
If and when the majority of people voted for it.

Wouldn't it take a lot of work to set up?
Yes, but once in place it would offer a more stable and fair system of democracy. As people become increasingly disillusioned with elected politicians, there is a growing international movement for direct democracy. The first question that needs answering is why democracies are failing their people. As you will see, in the UK the underlying problem is the lack of accountability to the electorate.

SECTION TWO

Horace Mop Head and the Green Gallstone

Horace Mop Head hated school trips almost as much as he hated the boiled cabbage sandwiches that his mother had made for his packed lunch. He lagged behind his classmates as the 'blue badge' guide lady elegantly swept them along through the corridors of Westminster.

'On the right-hand side we have the golden throne designed by Pugin, last used during the State Opening of Parliament. If you look carefully you will see figures of dragons and lions inlaid with gold leaf and emeralds,' she droned on.

As Horace stared at it he was sure one of the dragons was missing an eye. Then suddenly, the dragon winked at him with its other eye. Amazed, Horace popped a delicious piece of Blubber Muba bubble gum into his mouth and was softening it up nicely, with the intention of blowing a big pink sticky bubble. He was going to stick this on to the dragon's nose when no one was looking. What a laugh. He threw the wrapper on the floor, took a deep breath and stepped forward. One, two, three...

'You nasty little vermin,' shouted a man from behind him.

Horace jumped clean out of his sweaty nylon socks. A stern-looking security guard was standing over him, spit dribbling from the corner of his mouth. He was covered from head to foot in official-looking brass badges and tassels.

'I— I— I'm on a school trip,' spluttered Horace.

'Pick up your litter and move back to your group before I kick your fat butt into next week,' growled the guard rather impolitely.

Horace moved lightning fast and caught up with his classmates. He could see they were all staring at something that looked rather like a wooden stick. The blue badge guide commented in a rather high tone,

'Here we have the Lord Chancellor's wand, dating from the sixteenth century, it is used to fend off Black Rod at the State Opening of Parliament. It is not believed to have any inherent magical powers,' she peered down at a sea of vacant faces.

'If we now move along to we can see the murals painted with a bequeathal left by the Fourth Earl of Lardendripin.'

Horace hung back. He had a plan. 'Magic or not that wand must be worth a fortune,' he thought to himself. The wand sat on a brushed red velvet cushion and was protected by a small optical sensor. Waiting until he was alone, Horace took the sticky Blubber Muba bubble gum from his mouth and wedged it into the sensor. A moment later, as if by osmosis, the wand was in Horace's pocket.

Then to his amazement Horace heard a loud crack. Green smoke, mauve dust and yellow stars were whizzing around his head. As it cleared, Horace saw the most bizarre sight. Along the rows of green leather benches, various members of Parliament were now seated and Horace was sitting in the speaker's chair, with a large maroon robe draped over him. It was chaos.

MPs were arguing and throwing pieces of paper at each other, everyone was trying to speak at the same time, and all this was accompanied by howls of derision and cackles of laughter from the press gallery.

'You smelly old farts, you should all be burned,' shouted an inebriated journalist from the Daily Grumble, who was just about to fall off the balcony.

'What's going on?' said Horace, to a smart-looking usher standing next to him.

'It's parliamentary question time,' replied the usher.

What was really peculiar, was that along the rows of benches some of the members had twigs and leaves growing out of their ears.

'What's happened to them?' asked Horace.

'Oh that. Years ago, after the wicked Lord Marcher was expelled for bad behaviour he put a curse on the House of Commons. Now every time they say anything hypocritical they go green and sprout foliage. We have to prune the more serious cases.'

Horace thought this was all rather fine.

'Well I guess it taught them a lesson,' said Horace.

'Not really,' said the usher, 'they still argue but they tend to argue about different things, such as the price of fertiliser or whether organic is better than genetically modified. We've even had a few MPs who have been sent to the botanical gardens at Kew to recuperate.'

'Oh,' said Horace, as a spiky branch whisked past his head.

The usher added, 'The only thing that would break the curse is for someone to find the Green Gallstone and put it back in its rightful place.

'Where would that be?' said Horace.

'Nobody knows,' said the usher. 'Lord Marcher wouldn't tell us. It was his idea of a joke.'

After half an hour, Horace decided he needed a pee. He jumped down off the high chair and went looking for a toilet. In one of the dusty old corridors he found a room that had a large hand-painted sign upon it, which read,

GENTLEMEN'S WATER CLOSET WARNING:

then, in very bad Latin it read:

OBNOQNOCIOUS GASEOUS PERVASIVUS

He went inside and switched on the light, holding his nose as tightly as he could. Condensation was dripping from the ceiling and spiders were crawling everywhere. There were old copies of Private Eye magazine cut up neatly into squares and tied together on a piece of string. Suddenly the light went out and Horace could hear the door being locked from the outside. As he peered through the keyhole he could just see a figure dressed in cobalt blue, running away along the corridor.

There must be a key somewhere in here he thought. He climbed up and put his hand into the cistern. He could feel something slimy… but it wasn't a key. It was the Green Gallstone! As he held it above his head it seemed to glow in the dark. The door was still locked, so he squeezed himself through a small air vent and crawled along a tiny duct, until eventually his head appeared in the main chamber of the House of Commons.

'Help,' he squealed.

A tall MP, who was covered in cherry blossom, leaned over and lifted Horace down with one of his branches. Everyone in the chamber was amazed to see Horace holding the Green Gallstone.

'Well done, gorgeous,' said the cherry-blossomed MP.

The other MPs stood around Horace shaking his hand.

'Well done, my boy, but we still don't know where it came from originally,' another said.

Horace thought he knew. He found the one-eyed dragon and taking the sticky Blubber Muba bubble gum from his mouth, he pressed it into the dragon's eye socket. He then placed the Green Gallstone into position. Immediately there was a belching cloud of pink smoke and Horace found himself on the pavement outside the Houses of Parliament.

'Horace, we've been looking for you,' said the teacher.

The usher was standing over him.

'We think the lad had a knock on the head, he fell over in the toilet and banged his head. It must be mild concussion, he keeps talking about wands and toilet cisterns.'

'He's a little rascal. He's always getting into trouble,' complained the teacher.

'Look we must go, the coach is parked on double yellow lines and we're late.'

As Horace was helped on to the coach he took a final look back. He could hear the MPs shouting, and he was sure he could see the shadow of the handsomely wicked Lord Marcher staring at him from a window high in the Victorian building. Horace grinned and settled down for the long journey home. He'd had enough excitement for one day.

Chapter Two

A Beautiful Democracy

For an institution that legislates on law, the British Parliament at Westminster can seem rather complacent about its own behaviour. Westminster has always argued that being the highest court in the land it can supervise itself but this trust may be misplaced. Spin, sleaze, the system of Whips, expense abuses, secret lobbying, patronage, undeclared members' interests, party political sponsorship, fast tracking of career politicians, awards for political loyalty, patronage and political secrecy have all eroded the public's confidence in Parliament. Many people are now asking why politicians should have a different set of rules for themselves and the electorate they claim to represent?

What we would recognise is a political system that is corrupting, rather than the majority of MPs being inherently corrupt. Although, even politicians who have a high degree of integrity soon find themselves under pressure to accept the status quo. This suits those in power, who are invariably the only ones that can effect real change. Opposition parties frequently talk about reform then curiously loose any initiative once in power!

Turbulent times at Westminster

By 1996 John Major had been given the dubious honour of leading a Conservative government that had become known in the media as the 'party of sleaze,' after various irregular practices by Conservative

MP's came to light. Since 2001, Mr Blair's New Labour govern-ment has been labelled 'the party of spin' by the media. With an obsessive control over presentation and courting of the media, it has been hugely successful in the short term. In the long term, however, the British public have become sceptical of everything they are told. Has there been a deliberate attempt to manipulate the public's perception of government or was this an unforeseen consequence of a more dynamic administration? The answer appears to be yes to both of these questions.

Within two days of New Labour taking office, a meeting of privy councillors approved an order giving both Jonathan Powell and his then press secretary Alastair Campbell authority to instruct govern-ment civil servants[1] This overturned a long-standing parliamentary regulation that civil servants should be politically impartial. The appointment of so many special advisors, who had previously worked with New Labour, soon began to blur the distinction between elected politicians and civil servants. As Nicholas Jones pointed out, 'by December 2000, Mr Blair had authorised the appointment of seventy-nine politically appointed advisors... twen-ty six of them based at Number 10, three times as many as under John Major.[2] The salaries bill alone exceeded £4 million pounds[3] with Alastair Campbell commanding a salary of £96,275.

'In addition eighteen 'task force' groups were established to examine policy and a further eighty review bodies were formed to advise on a variety of diverse questions, including whether there were too many quangos (a type of bureaucratic administrative gov-ernment body)![4] As there already existed over 3,000 staff working in various press and information departments, these new layers of bureaucracy were difficult to justify. The taxpayer was unwittingly funding a government propaganda machine and there was no one to say they shouldn't. With such a huge New Labour majority in Parliament, it also became increasingly difficult for MPs to scrutinise all of the decisions that were being taken, many of them made in secret. Policies were increasingly presented as a fait accompli for parliamentary MPs to sign up to, or be sent into the political wilderness. Within Westminster's government, Select Committees remained one of the few ways in which government policy could effectively be scrutinised, but even here government interference began to increase.

Dr David Kelly

One of the main criticisms that led to the 2003 Hutton inquiry, into the death of the government scientist Dr David Kelly, was that he had leaked information despite government regulations. But in the year following Dr Kelly's premature death, it became clear that much of what Dr Kelly had claimed about Iraq's alleged 'weapons of mass destruction' was in fact true. Yet the New Labour government had itself leaked information over the preceding years, on various aspects of government policy.

Betty Boothroyd, the then speaker of the House of Commons, issued six official warnings against the government for disclosing information to the media, before it had been announced in the House of Commons[5] In July 2002, the Labour MP David Stewart resigned from the Scottish Affairs Select Committee after he admitted that he had been supplying extracts from reports to the then Secretary of State, the late Donald Dewar[6]

According to Westminster's own guidelines, any unauthorised use of unpublished Select Committee material is a 'contempt of Parliament'. Having access to copies of Select Committee reports, before they were published, meant the government could undermine any conclusions that were unpalatable before they had been made public. Andrew Marr, the BBC's political editor wrote,

'I would have, sat through weeks of compelling evidence-taking, followed by the release of a pungent, factually detailed and pointed report, only to see the whole thing dismissed by ministers... in a couple of bland lines.'[7]

Elizabeth Filkin, in her evidence to the Wick's committee, explained how she had received over 300 complaints on various aspects of parliamentary conduct by MPs during her term in office as Parliamentary Commissioner for Standards.

At the same time, government Whips became more involved with the appointment of Select Committee members. Eventually it became clear that Parliament was no longer able to scrutinise effectively its own legislation. As, Labour MP Dianne Abbott complained, 'The government see Select Committees as an irritant that must somehow be brought under their command and control structure.'[8]

Within our proposed system of direct democracy, a Code of Conduct and Ethics would be introduced which would include a range of new sanctions including: suspension without pay, and fines and imprisonment for serious offences such as fraud or bribery. The leaking of Select Committee documents would be made a disciplinary matter that would result in an MP being suspended for two months without pay. This Code would be overseen by an independent panel of senior judges, with the selection of Select Committee members given to a cross-party panel.

Another area that has caused much resentment among the public is that of MPs' remuneration and expenses. Since 1996, MPs have awarded themselves huge salary increases above the rate of inflation, while the general public and pensioners have struggled to survive on increases lower than real increases in the cost of living. In 2000, Gordon Brown offered pensioners an increase of 75p a week, until there was such a public outcry that it was increased to £2.20.[9]

So how much do MPs believe they are worth?

An MP's basic salary is now £56,358; the Prime Minister's is £171,554, the Lord Chancellor's £180,045, a cabinet minister's salary £124,979; the government Chief Whip's £124,979.[10]

However, many people are not aware that MPs can claim additional expenses worth up to £150,000 including:

- A staffing allowance of £71,310 for up to three members of staff (slightly less outside London).

- Incidental expenses of £18,799 to pay for computers, scanners and software.

- An additional £16,607 for MPs who are also devolved legislators or members of the European Parliament.

- A supplementary allowance of up to £1,574 if they have inner London seats.

- Or MPs can claim up to £20,333 for overnight accommodation if their constituencies are outside inner London.

- Funds are also available from the general services budget for training and insurance provision.

- MPs are given a mileage allowance of 56.1 pence per mile.

- A temporary staff allowance is available in cases where permanent staff are ill or on pregnancy leave.

- If MPs are called back to Parliament early there is a special contingency allowance to cover unanticipated costs.

- There's also a winding-up allowance, equivalent to one third of the staff allowance in the event of defeat, retirement or death.

- Then there's a resettlement grant for any MP who is not re-elected.

- Plus a severance payment of three months' salary if an MP loses a ministerial post.

- Prime Ministers are entitled to £72,310 for additional costs if they lose office.

- Finally, a generous pension scheme applies to all MPs, however long there term of reference.

And this does not take into account other earnings that MPs have outside of Parliament, relating to extra parliamentary activities such as speaking engagements. The members register of interests can be found at www.parliament.uk (this is a voluntary scheme and the information is incomplete!).

Contrast the above to an account given by Barbara Castle when she was working as an MP in the House of Commons in the 1940s:

'There was the view that it was a privilege to serve the public. You were underpaid and worked extraordinarily hard. The only perk you got was a free ticket to your constituency. We had no secretarial help in those days; nothing came out of the public funds to help us, no research assistant, no free postage.'[11]

Is it any wonder that the public are losing patience with today's career-minded politicians? In our model of direct democracy, any further pay, pension or expense increases for MPs would be linked to the rate of inflation and this would be set out within a parliamentary code. All expense claims would have to be audited and receipts kept as records for costs incurred. Once in place, these regulations could only be amended by the electorate, not by politicians.

Expense claims

In a system of direct democracy politicians would have to be made more accountable with regard to their expense claims, as some Westminster MPs seem to regard their expenses as entitlements. In December 2002, the Mail on Sunday published a story that alleged that Michael Trend had claimed the additional costs allowances for costs incurred while attending business in the House, despite the fact that he had driven home to Windsor on 'most evenings'. That amounted to an over claimant of £90,277.[12] The Commons eventually decided that he had 'acted negligently rather than with dishonest intent,' the recommended punishment was two weeks' suspension, with Trend agreeing to step down at the next general election. The question is whether a member of the public would have received such benign treatment, if they had done their sums wrong filling in their tax returns.

In the Scottish Parliament, Henry McLeish resigned as First Minister of Scotland after 'irregularities in his use of office costs allowance'[13] came to light. Cases like these are not exceptional. In Patrick Dixon's investigative book the The Truth About Westminster, he details a variety of abuses that have taken place on a regular basis, and it makes for worrying reading. An average of six cases of suspected 'misconduct' are uncovered every year by Westminster's House of Commons Fees Office yet no MP has ever been publicly named.[14] *At the same time, details of expenses that are claimed are not made available to the public.* This is hardly transparent or accountable.

What we would like to see introduced is a system whereby members have to keep accurate records of their expenses with receipts, (which would be audited by the Inland Revenue) and the results made available to the public. Why should businesses, charities and the public be fined for inaccurate or late filing of accounts, when Members of Parliament are under no legal obligation to even file audited accounts?

The ghost of self-regulation

Although the New Labour government produced a draft Corruption Bill in March 2003, later the same year in the Queen's Speech no mention was made of it. In the meantime, attempts at self-regulation by MPs have been lamentable. Andrew Mitchell was accused of attempting to influence the Chairman of the Members' Interests Committee during a parliamentary inquiry. Later the investigating committee 'concluded that neither Mitchell, as a government Whip, nor the Chairman should have engaged in an alleged conversation about the future of the inquiry.'[15] Later, David Willett's appointment to the Members' Interest Committee was criticised by the Standards and Privileges Committee.[16]

On various occasions the Parliamentary Commissioner for Standards reported difficulties with obtaining information from witnesses and explained that some of her investigators had been put under pressure from MPs during investigations. In the case of Keith Vaz - at that time a junior foreign officer minister - he was suspended from the House of Commons for one month due to his 'attempts to obstruct Filkin's investigations.'[17]

As Alex Salmond pointed out when talking about the appointment of the new Parliamentary Commissioner for Standards, Sir Philip Mawer:

'All these people, regardless of how honourable they are and how diligently they carry out their duties, are none the less politicians regulating other politicians. It is impossible for people wholly to remove themselves from the political process when they are active politicians.'[18]

The second chamber – the House of Lords

So, do such abuses only occur in the House of Commons? The Daily Telegraph newspaper ran a story, which highlighted the fact that 654 Lords were now claiming annual expenses in the region of £34 million. In the House of Lords, one peer described how:

'a Commons' researcher had come to him in great distress, as it had come to his attention that ten well-known members of the House of Lords had apparently been claiming daily attendance allowances worth thousands of pounds, for periods when they were not at the House.'[19]

The problem is that very few people within government are prepared to speak out. Some Lords work very long hours and don't claim any expenses but why should their reputations be sullied by others who abuse the system? Some peers have even taken to signing in then leaving without doing any work, in order to receive a full expenses allowance.[20] One of our aims would be to ensure that members of the House of Lords would only receive expenses if they completed a full day's work and had been signed in and out (under security regulations, hours of attendance already have to be recorded). As with MPs, the Lords would also be expected to prepare yearly audited accounts that would be available for public scrutiny.

Be My Whipper-in Boy

The basic principle of representative democracy is that MPs are supposed to represent their constituents, but the UK has within its parliamentary system, politicians who are known as Whips (the title Whips comes from the word 'whipper-in', a hunt official who uses a whip to manage hounds). The Whip's job is to discipline other MPs, but MPs who vote against the wishes of their party leadership soon find themselves facing the anger of these Whips. The Whips have enormous power within government but few people realise what they do. As one MP said:

> 'Most people outside Parliament, don't realise how influential the Whips are in advancing the careers of Members of Parliament. The 'right' people can be judiciously advanced up the greasy pole of promotion by the Whips.'[21]

Essentially, the Whips tell MPs when their support is required and how they should vote. By assigning a one-, two- or three-line Whip, it indicates what priority the government has assigned to any piece of legislation. We have even had accounts of Whips contacting the wives of MPs to 'persuade' their husbands how to vote and it is not unknown for Whips to force MPs who are on their deathbed into the House to vote.[22]

The importance that government places on the position, is reflected in the Chief Whip's salary of £124,979. More than double that of most MPs.[23] *The question is how can an MP represent his voters with this sort of interference?* Few MPs are prepared to face the wrath of their Whips and those who do usually lose their jobs. Teresa Gorman, a Conservative politician, described what happened when she made a stand against unpopular government policies, including intimidation and sexual abuse. She recounts what happened when two government Whips intimidated her during a debate.

The first Whip said, 'A woman's place is in the home.'

'Yes, flat on her back,' the next said.

The first Whip said, 'Women should be barefoot and pregnant. They shouldn't be let in here in the first place.'[24]

Both government and opposition Whips have a series of measures that they can use to 'persuade' MPs including: honours; awards; invitations to Buckingham Palace; receptions at Downing Street; quango appointments; the promise of safer parliamentary seats; promise of ministerial appointments; and trips abroad. The difficulty is that these politicians are supposedly voting on behalf of the public. Within direct democracy, 'whipping' and any similar practices would be banned.

Vote with us – or resign!

Whipping is just one of the ways MPs are manipulated when voting; another is the 'payroll vote', also known as 'collective cabinet responsibility'. Government ministers have to vote with the government, unless they are prepared to resign or be be sacked. As ministerial responsibility 'implies that all cabinet ministers assume responsibility for cabinet decisions and actions to implement those decisions,'[25] ministers have to vote with the government.

Originally the convention only applied to senior ministers but it has been extended to include junior ministers and parliamentary private secretaries. During their terms as Prime Minister, both James Callaghan and Harold Wilson forced ministers to sack parliamentary private secretaries after they refused to vote with the government.[26] When you have ministers earning £70,000 more than an MP, it is quite an incentive not to step out of line.

What many people don't realise is that collective cabinet responsibility now extends to over 140 MPs, whereas in 1900 there were only thirty, who were tied to this convention.[27] Many have been promised senior appointments in government but how can they be expected to represent their constituents if they are not free to vote? Direct democracy would also ensure that collective cabinet responsibility be banned outside of the immediate cabinet.

One for you, one for me

Lobbying might be thought of as 'the hidden hand of influence' within government, but it is a questionable practise within a genuine democracy. In 1997, based on the register of MPs interests, 171 MPs[28] were acting as consultants or advisors to outside interests, with 62 being employed by more than one company.[29] Although lobbying companies argue in public that they don't have much influence, why are they prepared to spend so much on political lobbying if it is so ineffective? So what do we know about these lobbying groups?

For lobbying to be effective it is often targeted at the pre-legislative stage of any bill, including Standing Committees, when MPs are asked to 'table amendments'. As Steve John, who widely researched the subject discovered, 'lobbyists can be effective if they use high-profile tactics to increase the salience of the issue within government.'[30] He noted that during the 1980s, 39 MPs were part owners of lobbying companies and many MPs had themselves been professional lobbyists before entering Parliament.[31] In 1987 a Westminster Select Committee concluded that:

> 'there is increasing lobbying activity in Westminster, that it will continue to increase, and that conflicts of interest will more frequently confront MPs.'[32]

Surely MPs leave themselves open to criticism if what they are supposed to be doing first and foremost is representing their constituents. Effective lobbying is far from transparent as: 'a great lobbyist is like the perpetrator of the perfect crime.'[33] By their nature they are discreet about their practices. One company calling itself the Public Policy Unit once described itself as made up of:

> 'former officials, ministers, MPs, peers and political advisors, who now act as policy analysts and consultants on dealing with political and regulatory bodies at central and local government levels in the United Kingdom and EC.'[34]

Lobbying firms don't just represent companies or corporations. Records exist to show that foreign governments have employed lobbying companies to gain influence in Westminster. The Azerbaijan Republic, the State of Bahrain and the British Virgin Islands are just some of the documented examples. One prominent lobbying group was even employed by the Chilean Reconciliation Movement to campaign for the release of General Pinochet after the British authorities held him.[35]

Cash for Questions

In 1994 two undercover reporters working for the Sunday Times posed as businessmen and found that of only ten MPs questioned, two of them, Graham Riddick and David Tredinnick were prepared to take cash to ask specific questions in Parliament.[36] It was some of these concerns that triggered the Lord Nolan inquiry over standards in Westminster in 1994. The eventual investigation was so embarrassing that government meetings were held in private until Tony Benn published his own transcripts and was expelled from the Committee. Although Lord Nolan's extensive and detailed report made a variety of recommendations, the measures that were introduced fell short of the original recommendations.

In the 1990s, Lord Nolan found that that 30 per cent of all Westminster MPs were being paid for by consultancies for advice and lobbying. As was reported in The Times, 'In the mid-1980s many of the MPs who were defending BA's commercial interests were said to be receiving benefits worth thousands of pounds.'[37] Some lobbying companies did make attempts at self-regulation. Such as Ian Greer's company (no longer trading) that had represented clients such as British Airways, Cadbury Schweppes and Prime Minister Bhutto, but many lobbying companies are highly secretive.[38]

Political lobbying is now a worldwide phenomenon. In the United States, political lobbying has reached astronomical proportions. As Anthony Barnett writes,

> 'United States voters are realistically cynical about the financial corruption of politics. Aware that no one can run for office without television adverts and that no one can afford these without massive fundraising, they see correctly that politics in their country has been irredeemably bought by money.'[39]

Lobbying groups are also hard at work within the European Union (EU), covering subjects as wide ranging as pharmaceuticals, road building and education programmes. Within the EU there is a pervading culture of 'influence' but as we shall see the EU does not have the effective checks needed to curtail its abuse.

In our model for direct democracy in the UK, we would propose that all the recommendations from Lord Nolan's and Lord Neill's reports on parliamentary standards be put into place, including compulsory declarations in a register of members' interests. A new Code of Ethics would be set up by a completely independent judicial body with severe sanctions against those who failed to comply.

The independence of the Parliamentary Commissioner for Standards also needs to be reinforced or we may well face the same situation that Elizabeth Filkin, the Parliamentary Commissioner for Standards faced. Despite enormous public support for her investigations into the ethical standards of parliament, she was not reappointed. The Guardian newspaper suggested that she had been:

'too effective and that MPs would like to replace her with someone who might give them a slightly more comfortable ride.'[40]

Is that a gong?

Questionable practise has taken place in another area of the UK's democracy. It comes under the general heading of patronage and involves the handing out of prestigious awards, appointments and key positions within government. The British system of honours was developed from the practice of medieval kings awarding 'honours' in return for favours done by their nobles. After the First World War, honours had not only become a way of confirming loyalty over controversial political issues, it was also a means of financing political parties.

Lloyd George's coalition party of Liberals and Conservatives financed many of its activities by selling peerages and knighthoods. New honours were even introduced, such as the OBE (Order of the British Empire), to extract money for political funds from those who could not afford more expensive donations. By 1922 this developed into a full-scale scandal, when politicians such as Sir John Drughorn (convicted for trading with the enemy in 1915), Sir William Vestey (tax evasion) and Sir Joseph Robinson (a South African fraudster) were found to have bought their positions in the House of Lords.[41] There was little exposure in the press, as Lloyd George had made sure that the largest newspaper proprietors had all received free peerages. Coincidentally, Max Aitken the newspaper mogul became Lord Beaverbrook only two days after Lloyd George became Prime Minister in 1916.

Decisions about who is to receive honours are made in secret by the Prime Minister and the Chief Whip (originally known as the Patronage Secretary) and the discussions take place in private. The Sunday Times printed an article quoting an unnamed company secretary, whose chairman was knighted following a donation of £160,000 to a political party. She said, 'It was made perfectly clear beforehand that if he did this, he would get a knighthood.'[42] Unfortunately, these practices devalue something that could be a way of rewarding genuine merit. Some of these politically appointed honours even give entitlement to those who receive them, to sit in the House of Lords, where legislation is scrutinised.

In our model for direct democracy we would like to see the honours system and its equivalents taken out of the hands of politicians and given to an independent panel. We would also propose to limit the number of politicians to receive honours and instead award them to members of the public chosen by the public. Each county could honour a local person who had shown an outstanding commitment to their region or local community. They could be doctors, charity workers or street cleaners, but the public would have the right to choose.

Would you be my quango?

The acronym 'quango', which stands for quasi-autonomous non-governmental organisation, was first used by the writer Anthony Barker. It is essentially a British administrative body, usually nominated rather than elected. Quango's now control billions of pounds of taxpayers' money, with little accountability for their actions. In the mid 1980s, during Mrs Thatcher's drive to centralise British government, these quangos took over many roles that local councils used to fulfil. *The problem is one of accountability, for their decisions are often made in private and the public has no control over the decisions that they make.*

The Democratic Audit of Britain discovered that there were now 5,521 executive quangos in the UK responsible for around one third of all public spending[43] describing these quangos as:

> 'a complex jumble of public bodies, private companies, voluntary outfits and others operating under no consistent regime of constitutional or legal accountability.'[44]

Examples of quangos range from the Housing Corporation which spends around £1.8 billion, to the National Rivers Authority with over 7500 staff, plus other more obscure quangos, such as the UK Polar Medal Assessment Committee, the Indian Family Pension Funds Body of Commissioners and the Advisory Committee on Novel Foods and Processes.[45] Many of these bodies meet in secret. For instance MAFF (what was the Ministry of Agriculture) has a committee on toxicity classification of food - such as looking into what might or might not be put into vitamin pills. The committee 'meets in secret and is not obliged to give any reasons for its conclusions.'[46]

Many quangos in turn complain of the proliferation of bureaucracy from central government, with a complex duplication of forms, applications, reports, targets, policy statements, directives, schedules, memos and enquiries streaming down from central government. Unfortunately, this bureaucratic chaos has produced some rather poor results. West Midlands regional health authority in England was criticised by auditors after wasting £10m because of 'serious shortcomings in the management, control and accountability of services.'[47] One senior civil servant more candidly described it as 'a shambles.'[48] The suspicion was that rather too many people were using 'networking' to arrange deals that fell short of acceptable practices.

Later a story appeared in The Independent Newspaper, by the reporter Christian Wolmar, which drew attention to a report by the Commons Public Accounts Committee. This criticised the way in which the Department of Transport had sold off railway depots as businesses with a cash balance of £1 million, when they actually had £17 million in 'liquid' reserves. The result was that £13 million of taxpayers' money was never recovered. The Department of Transport even attempted to classify many of the relevant documents - no one was publicly held accountable. On the same day in the business section of the newspaper Chris Godsmark wrote an article reporting that John Prideaux, 'a former senior board director of British Rail,' received an unspecified windfall consideration through a complex deal, in which one of those involved was believed to have netted £36 million.'[49]

In recent years, there has been so much disquiet about quangos that various governments have attempted to reduce their numbers. One innovative way of doing this was to change their names! In one fell swoop thousands of quangos were removed from the official list only to reappear as NGOs (non-governmental organisations), EGOs (extra government organisations), NDPBs (non-departmental public bodies), Task Force Groups and other useful acronyms. This failed to mask the fact that the number of 'quango' type administrative bodies was still increasing.

'Can I call a friend?'

So can the public be confident that suitable people are chosen to head up these prestigious organisations? Surely potential candidates are taken from the best applicants, thoroughly vetted and put through the most rigorous of procedures, are experts in their field and have a proven track record of their ability to control billion pound budgets? The answer is not really. Patronage in Britain has spread into public life in a way that the Soviet Bloc commissars would have been proud of. Put another way, the British taxpayer has been 'quangoed'. By 1994 quangos were responsible for £60 billion pounds of public money, almost one third of the government's total expenditure and many quango appointments came with generous salaries, pensions and expenses packages.

Michael Griffith managed to gain five appointments earning an extra £57,313 on top of his salary.[50] Was he really an expert in conservation, higher education, the NHS, libraries and the countryside? His explanation when challenged was that 'once you do a bit of public work, you get known.'[51] On another occasion a chairman of a quango was appointed 'following a pheasant shoot at which the Secretary of State was a fellow gun.'[52] Many of these appointments are highly lucrative. For example, Lord Wyatt of Weeford was appointed to chair the Horserace Totalisator Board on a salary of £95,000 a year.[53]

In the UK the government body that officially oversees such appointments is known as the Public Appointments Unit, although in the majority of cases it is the relevant government department that chooses.[54] British government ministers now have the authority to give away 51,000 public appointments, with 10,000 new appointments expected over the next couple of years. Incredibly, the Government's Chief Whips office is allowed to vet any politically significant appointments. The Economist magazine declared that: 'Power Ministers are taking for themselves, they are giving to their friends'. On one occasion the Chairman of the Tourist Board: 'was not asked a single question about his plans, nor was anyone else interviewed, before he was given the job by phone.'[55]

Baroness Denton was infamously quoted as saying, 'I can't remember knowingly appointing a Labour supporter,' she later justified this with, 'you don't put in people who are in conflict with what you are trying to achieve.'[56] If all this were only about friends having a chat over a drink, people wouldn't mind. The problem is that billions of pounds of taxpayers' money is sloshing around a large bureaucratic trough with rather too many snouts deeply buried in it! So how accountable are these organisations? Stuart Weir, a researcher on the subject, discovered that only one third of these quangos were accountable to the two main government auditing bodies, only 14 per cent were covered by an ombudsman and only 5 per cent allowed members of the public to attend their meetings.[57]

The UK's democracy now has a non-accountable bureaucracy built into its very core that is out of control. One journalist who researched these bodies - asked the poignant question: What sense is there:

> 'for the state to gather it all up, pass it around, eventually confess that it doesn't really know how to spend it and then pass it back, but only to people who are locally anonymous and operate in small discrete groups.'[58]

As the Adam Smith Institute pointed out:

> 'Ministers have discovered that the system can be used for shedding personal responsibility, rewarding friends, expanding the corporate state, diminishing the authority of Parliament... On its present scale, the vast and complex network of quangos encourages an abuse of patronage and invites corruption.'[59]

The corporate face of government

Together with the rise of personal patronage, we have also seen an alarming increase in the influence of large corporations within government. Many of us now rely on the various companies that produce the goods and services that we enjoy but what role should they be allowed to play in a democracy? George Monbiot in his book, Captive State, found 43 examples of senior corporate executives being given influential positions within government. Here are just some of the examples:

- Lord Marshall of Knightsbridge, the Chairman of British Airways - who campaigned against proposals to introduce aviation tax aimed at reducing the damaging affects of climate change - put in charge of Gordon Brown's energy tax review, which investigated the case for new fuel taxes on corporations, with the aim of reducing their contribution to global warming.[60]

- Ewen Cameron - President of the County Landowners Association, where he fought against the government's plans for a right to roam - became Chairman of the government's Countryside Agency, responsible for implementing the right to roam.[61]

- Lord Simon of Highbury - the Chairman of BP, the international oil and gas company which lobbied against oil taxation (Lloyd's List, 26 November 1996) and Vice Chairman of the European Round Table of Industrialists, a lobby group which drafted the Single European Act - made Minister for Trade and Competitiveness in Europe, at the Department of Trade and Industry. Responsible for negotiating a common energy tax with the EU.[62]

- Jack Cunningham MP - paid advisor to Albright and Wilson (UK), an agrochemical company and member of the Chemical Industries Association, which lobbies for the deregulation of pesticides - made Secretary of State for Agriculture and Chair of the Cabinet committee on biotechnology, which co-ordinates government policy on pesticides.[63]

- Ian McAllister - Chairman and Managing Director Ford UK. Until December 1999 Ford was a member of the Global Climate Coalition, which lobbies against attempts to reduce carbon dioxide emissions - made Chairman of the government's Cleaner Vehicles Task Force.[64]

- Professor Peter Schroeder - Director of Research Nestlé - became Director of the government's Institute of Food Research.[65]

It is not unreasonable that companies attempt to advance their interests but how can a democratic system justify having such people so close to the heart of the government, where there are such clear conflicts of interest. What this shows is that corporations,

> 'with the British government's blessing, (corporations) have begun to develop a transatlantic single market controlled and run by corporate chief executives.'[66]

The needs of corporations are not necessarily incompatible with the wishes of the electorate but we would be naïve to believe that the needs of the electorate are a top priority for private corporations. *First and foremost, corporations have a duty to their shareholders not the public.*

Worse, they remain largely unaccountable and secretive regarding the influence they have over elected governments. In many other countries the problem is far worse, where many political parties are largely funded with money from international corporations.

Conclusion

The UK's democracy needs overhauling and there are many people who agree. Not least the many MPs who recognise the failings of the system. Betty Boothroyd the highly respected speaker of the House of Commons retired in July 2000 after forty years service. Her closing speech expressed some of her concerns, when she said, 'effective scrutiny and the democratic process must take priority over the conveniences of members.'[67] *The problem is that none of the major political parties have anything to gain from change but the electorate are receiving a very poor deal.* So how is it that two political parties, with a relatively small membership, have managed to successfully dominate British politics for nearly one hundred years? In the UK, as elsewhere, the answer is money, and lots of it.

Chapter Three

Pulling the Strings of Power

New Labour has a membership of 248,294 individual members. It is estimated that the Conservative Party has a membership of around 160,000 (although they will not publicly disclose the information). The Conservatives seem to have a problem in confirming their figures; at the last count many Conservative Social Club members were included, even though apparently, many had only joined the local Conservative clubs 'for the cheap beer!'[1] The National Trust charity has seven times more members than both the Conservatives and New Labour added together, with just over 3.3 million members. So what about the finances of these political parties?

By 1991 the Conservative Party was £12 million in debt and was spending far more money than it was generating.[2] Then again, in 2001, it is believed that the Conservative Party was close to bankruptcy. In 2003, the accountants Pricewaterhouse Coopers refused to sign off the Conservative Party's own accounts saying, 'there is not enough income to guarantee the party's viability.[3] At the same time New Labour has only managed to avoid bankruptcy by relying on its substantial overdraft facility, after their accounts revealed a deficit of £8.9 million in 2001.[4] Yet at the last election the Conservatives and New Labour between them managed to spend an estimated £38 million and during any parliamentary term there are other elections that have to be paid for.[5] So where does all this money come from? As you will see political fundraising is not always as ethical or transparent as we are led to believe.

Lack of transparency

On 23 February 1995, the Register of Members' Interests showed that both Tony Blair and Gordon Brown had received funding from an organisation called the Industrial Research Trust, overseen by Lord Grigson.[6] The money almost certainly came from trade unions but the identities of the donors were masked by passing it through various 'front' organisations.[7] When Tony Blair was elected party leader in 1994, his personal campaign budget was around £80,000. This was twice as much as his nearest rival but he refused to say from where the money originated. It was conjectured that it was from various trade unions.[8]

It is worth noting that after all the complaining from New Labour over secret Conservative funding during the election campaign, they were doing the same themselves. After the election an article appeared in The Independent newspaper revealing that New Labour had laundered anonymous funds via a front company called Common Campaigns Ltd, with both Lord Haskel and Lord Clinton-Davis as directors.[9]

Loads of money

And New Labour has managed to raise funds from other intriguing sources:

- There was a donation of £50,000 from Paul Drayson, the owner of a company called Powderject Pharmaceuticals. Soon after this, Powderject Pharmaceuticals won a government contract worth £32 million to supply vaccines that would 'protect Britain against a bio-terrorist attack.'[10] The government claimed that Powderject 'was the only company that could produce quickly the millions of doses needed.'[11] Until, of course, it came to light that other British companies could have met the order more cheaply, such as Acambis of Cambridge, who were already in the process of manufacturing 210 million doses of vaccine for the US government.[12]

Although questions were raised in Parliament, the government's response was that standard procurement procedures were 'waived in the interests of national security'. The government failed to come up with a convincing explanation as to why the Acambis vaccine was unsuitable.

- In June 2001 a businessmen called Lakshmi Mittal, whose interests were based solely overseas, donated £125,000 to New Labour. Following this, the Prime Minister personally intervened on Mittal's behalf to encourage the Romanian Government to use Mittal's steel in a huge construction order in Romania. Although ministers argued that it was done to support British industry, Mittal's company was, in fact, registered in Holland and it had been competing against other British steel manufacturers who desperately needed the work.[13]

- In 1997 Bernie Ecclestone (Sir Bernie Ecclestone), the Formula One racing boss, donated £1 million to New Labour to help them with their election campaign.[14] Shortly after Mr Blair became Prime Minister, New Labour retracted its pledge to ban all tobacco advertising and made an exception to Formula One racing. Mr Blair then appeared on the television programme *On the Record* and with a straight face insisted that the donation 'had no influence on the government's decision to exempt Formula One racing from the sponsorship ban.'[15]

- In 1997 The Telegraph newspaper reported that despite the Labour Party's stated opposition to out-of-town shopping centres, Labour had apparently softened its stance with regards to planning permission. Following a parliamentary question, John Prescott confirmed that a meeting had been held with Lord Sainsbury, which had covered 'mixed-use housing and retail development and the speed and consistency of the planning process generally.' Lord Sainsbury, who had been nominated by Tony Blair for a peerage, had reputedly donated £1 million to the Labour Party.[16]

- In 2001 allegations were made against Peter Mandelson that he had 'made inquiries on behalf of the Hinduja brothers and intervened (in respect of their passport application) in a manner that was neither his departmental, nor his constituency responsibility. The Hinduja brothers had donated £1 million to the Labour Party.'[17]

- Things really got sticky for New Labour when it was discovered that it had accepted a donation from the giant power company Enron.[18] The same Enron that was later to become embroiled in the largest corporate fraud case in American corporate history, with some of its directors now in jail.[19] No one has yet explained what an American oil company was hoping to gain by donating to a British political party?

People, unions and businesses should be free to give to political parties. The question is whether this money is buying an unfair influence on political decisions. Would for instance Mrs Noggin from Pontefract, who is worried about the leaking roof at her daughter's school, be able to arrange a short-notice meeting with the Prime Minister? It seems doubtful unless she has very deep pockets.

The Labour Party

The Labour Party has always had a very close bond with British Trade Unions. Labour would not exist today unless it had been given Trade Union support both politically and financially over the years. Many unions do an excellent job for their members and are, of course, entitled to exert influence where they can. The question is how can New Labour claim to represent the whole nation and at the same time reconcile that with the demands made by their largest financial backers, the unions? The structure of the Labour Party is made up of affiliated trade unions, socialist societies and constituent memberships. Individual members were only accepted into the Labour Party thirty years after its inception in 1918.[20]

At the same time, it is not individual members who have control over what the money is spent on. If a union wants to give money to the Labour Party, its individual members do have the right to opt out of the political levy, *but they have to request it.*[21] In 1995 over half of Labour's income of £12.5 million was provided by the unions[22] As Lord Healey pointed out, 'without union money in many cases we could not run election campaigns. The unions do expect a return for it.'[23] This quote was rather telling. So the unions don't hand over cash from the goodness of their own hearts? It has not been unknown for unions to threaten the withdrawal of sponsorship from MPs who seem to oppose union official policy.[24]

The inner workings of Labour

The point that individuals have little control over what happens is vividly illustrated by rules relating to Conference - the main decision-making body of the Labour Party. *It is 'Conference' that controls and administers the workings of the Labour Party.* Most importantly it decides on 'specific proposals of legislative, financial or administrative reform which shall be included in the party programme.'[25] The National Executive Committee is expected to provide guidance for Conference on policy, but it is the Conference that votes whether to accept it or not. Half of the National Executive Committee is made up of affiliated trade unions, with an extra seat kept for socialist societies. The trade unions also have half the votes at Conference and one third of the votes, when electing a party leader and a deputy leader.[26]

Trade Unions affiliated to Labour are entitled to a number of delegates, based on the size of their affiliation and therefore how much funding they bring. The Labour Party structure seems complex because it was restructured in 1900 following the decision by the House of Lords to establish working-class representation in Parliament. This saw the coming together of various class bodies such as the Trade Unions and other socialist organisations. However, we need to remember that when a union chooses to affiliate to the Labour Party, it is the union that affiliates not the individual members of the union. In fairness to the Labour administration, they have attempted to introduce some restrictions on their own funding arrangements.

In contrast, the Conservative Party makes the antics of New Labour look rather amateurish. In Colin Challen's book, *Price of Power*, he details some of the secret funding that has come to light over the years.[27] Considering this is only what we are aware of, it reads like a best-selling thriller.

- Asil Nadir, the head of the Polly Peck empire, claimed he had donated £365,000 to Conservative party funds via a National Westminster Bank account in Jersey.[28] Nadir said that he later gave another million pounds. This might have upset some of Polly Peck's shareholders; they lost almost everything after the Serious Fraud Squad started investigating Mr Nadir's financial arrangements. The company's administrator Touche Ross found that the donation had been 'misappropriated,' but the Conservative Party refused to hand the money back claiming, 'it had not been proven that it was actually stolen'.[29]

Around the same time Business Age magazine discovered that the meteoric rise of the Polly Peck company was not, in fact, built on tins of canned fruit but arms trading between both sides of the Iran-Iraq conflict.[30] Nadir was eventually charged with eighteen offences of theft and false accounting, amounting to £25 million. After he was bailed for £3.5 million (a bizarrely low sum considering the amounts of money involved) Nadir jumped bail and fled to Northern Cyprus.

• Then there's the case of Octav Botnar. It was claimed he donated £150,000 to the Conservatives, with money deposited into a bank account in Jersey at the 'suggestion of Conservative party officials who preferred this to a less confidential donation.'[31] Before an arrest warrant was issued for tax fraud totalling £97 million, Botnar fled Britain via Switzerland. By 1996 the Inland Revenue was claiming £230 million from Mr Botnar's assets, although they could only locate £80 million. Botnar had wisely transferred £250 million into a Liechtenstein Bank account.[32]

• Nazmu Virani, who was eventually jailed in May 1994 for his part in the collapse of the Bank of Credit and Commerce International, admitted giving substantial donations to the Conservative Party over many years.[33]

• Arms' dealer Mohamad Hashemi claimed to have donated £85,000 to the Conservative Party. This only came to light after the Serious Fraud Squad had raided his premises and he began to protest about how well connected he was politically![34]

- Conservative parliamentary candidate John Kennedy had 'close connections' to the Serb leader Radovan Karadzic. According to the *Sunday Times*, he passed on a donation of £50,000 to the Conservative Party. As we know Karadzic was later indicted on war crimes.[35]

- There was Giovanni Di Stefano, the foreign affairs spokesman for Zelijko Raznatovic, who had owned a variety of businesses in the United Kingdom. He admitted that he had directed tens of thousands of pounds to the Conservative Party, shortly before completing three years of a prison sentence for fraudulent trading.[36] Afterwards, he returned to Yugoslavia and was later described by the Sunday Times as helping to organise a 'ruthless paramilitary unit accused of genocide in Bosnia'.[37]

- There was John Latsis the Greek shipping magnate who donated £2 million to Conservative party funds.[38] It later came to light that he was, in fact, a 'foreign domicile'. This meant that while he was living in the UK he only had to pay tax on earnings that the Inland Revenue could prove he had earned in the UK.[39]

- The merchant bank Hambros, which appeared to do so well from rail privatisation and the sale of Ministry of Defence Housing, was discovered to have donated £368,000 to the Tories (Lord Hambro had been Conservative party treasurer).[40]

- In 1979 a consortium called Electra Fleming bought Her Majesty's Stationery Office for the mysteriously 'low price of less than £54 million.'[41] At the same time another business consortium that had offered £65 million had their bid rejected. The government gave the reason for rejecting the higher bid as being 'less well defined.'[42] It later came to light that the winning consortium included Robert Fleming Bankers and Electra Investment Trust plc, who had altogether contributed around £567,000 to Conservative funds. [43]

- At one point when Conservative party debts showed that in strict accounting terms they were - on paper - bankrupt, they were, fortunately, able to secure an overdraft facility with the Bank of Scotland for around £15 million.[44] The Royal Bank of Scotland at the time just happened to be chaired by Lord Younger, the former Conservative Party Chairmen. This might have upset some small businesses and homeowners who banked with the Royal Bank of Scotland. At the time property repossessions and bankruptcies were soaring.

- Multifarious donations were made by directors of various utilities companies that had benefited so much from the series of government privatisations.

Of course, the Conservative Party has always had close links with business and it's not within the remit of this book to try and cover all the cases. These are already well documented and it would have meant running to over three volumes! But for some Conservative MPs it was all too much. Emma Nicholson MP deserted the Conservatives and joined the Liberal Party declaring of the Conservatives:

'their cloak of superiority had been stripped away to reveal the greed beneath. Among those who opposed the vote on limited disclosure, some were already rich who wanted to get richer,' they were 'greedy above their worth to Parliament'[45]

Financial Creativity

The Conservative Party should have received a golden globe award for their fundraising efforts, as their creativity seemed to know no bounds. In 1995 Labour MP Barry Sheerman discovered that the Conservative Party was raising half a million pounds a year by pitching direct mailings to wealthy businessmen. He says, 'I first became aware of this scam when I saw a mass mail-out of the Conservative Party Team 1000… which implied that entertainment at the Palace of Westminster was clearly one of the perks.'[46] This entertainment included the use of Westminster's dining facilities. A facility that was intended for the sole use of MPs to cater for their constituents and guests. This stretched the definition of 'guests' a little too far.

During that period Conservative MPs had made 1,399 bookings compared to Labour's 167, netting them a cool half a million pounds.[47] Well why not? The facilities were free. Free that is to MPs but all paid for by the taxpayer. Then the Conservative Party devised something called the Premier Club that charged guests '£100,000 a year for the pleasure of being able to share access to the Prime Minister.'[48] Shortly afterwards John Beckworth's property consortium was shortlisted to bid for the privatisation of Ministry of Defence housing.

John Beckworth just happened to be the Premier Club's Chairman. Eventually, William Haig, the new leader of the Conservative Party, decided to call a halt to the financial shenanigans but he had no idea of the extent of it all. Michael Ashcroft, who couldn't spend more than 90 days in the UK[49] unless he wanted to pay British taxes, quietly donated £1 million to the Conservative Party election fund from a trust set up in Belize, Central America.[50] At the time he was also Conservative party treasurer who was supposed to be overseeing the parliamentary guideline that all foreign donations were banned.

At least it's not the taxpayers' money

You might argue that strange things can happen in politics but that the parties should be free to raise funds however they wish. It is not as though the taxpayer is funding them. Wrong! After a series of public consultations, showing quite clearly that the public had no wish or desire to fund political parties, *in 1975 a system for the state funding of political parties was introduced*. It uses the loophole of political research and development but it amounts to the same thing. The system is called 'Short Money,' and although funded by the taxpayer, it is used to develop political party policy. Surely you'd think this money would be allocated to the parties that have the lowest income, parties that might begin to address some democratic inequalities? Wrong!

During 1998 the Conservative Party received £986,762; the Liberals £371,997; and the Unionists £45,867.[51] Seeing that these larger parties already have funds far in excess of smaller parties, this again tilts the balance of power in their favour. *It also means that as a taxpayer you are supporting various political parties even when you fundamentally disagree with them*. You would think that this must have appeared in one of the political party manifestos, so that the electorate would have been made aware of this novel approach to political funding. Wrong again! I'm afraid you were left in the dark because it appears that that is the only safe place for the public to stay!

Conclusion

Over the last few years, two important reports were compiled relating to financial and ethical standards in Parliament. The first was the Nolan report and the second was Lord Neill's report into ethics. Even though a great deal of time and care were given to these reports, the government simply waited for public anger to die down and then a few weak measures were introduced that have had relatively little effect. We would propose putting into place both Lord Nolan's and Lord Neill's recommendations in full, together with the following measures:

- Donations from non-UK voters, or non-UK registered companies or foreign governments or foreign trusts would not only be banned but a confiscation of the funds and severe fines would be applied to any party breaking the regulations.

- A limit of £10 million would be placed on election expenditure for each party (adjusted against the rate of inflation); audited accounts of election campaigns would be published by independent auditors.

- A records of donors who make donations above £1,000 would be published.

- All political donations (whatever the amount) from public companies (and unions) would have to be approved by all shareholders (or members) with a vote. The regulatory body that oversees Parliamentary Codes and Ethics would oversee this and impose effective sanctions against any party that did not abide by the rules. In cases of irregularities, fines would be calculated as a percentage of the sums involved.

- Affiliated party memberships to political parties would be abandoned, as it was in Sweden in 1990, and Norway in 1997.[52]

- In strict legal terms, political parties are voluntary associations but in practice they have become semi-public bodies that go beyond the immediate needs of their members. Therefore access to ministers by those who supporting the political parties (whether individuals or companies) would be regulated.

- All political parties would have to become limited companies and have the same conditions for auditing applied to them, that limited companies presently have. These accounts would have to be independently audited on a yearly basis by the Inland Revenue and made available to the public.

Chapter Four

✔

Monarchy & Parliament

The normal response from MPs when challenged over parliamentary shortcomings is to argue that 'things have always been done this way.' Not only is that a poor excuse, it is also untrue! If we look back over history what we find is a struggle between various political groups, all attempting to gain as much power as possible. Occasionally, scandal has threatened Parliament's power base but it has never shown an appetite for widening its democratic remit. *The electorate has so little influence now because they never were intended to have any influence.*

The rights that people do now have were often secured by individuals who risked their lives struggling against inherent inequalities. Moreover, the development of British democracy has had profound consequences on the development of democracies all around the world. The problem is that representative democracy is firmly based on eighteenth century practices that can hardly be expected to meet the needs of the electorate into the twenty-first century. So how did representative democracy develop and why has it become a model for countries all over the world?

The fall of the monarchy – the rise of Parliament

By 1625 Charles I, son of King James I, had been crowned King of England. As with many English monarchs, Charles needed money to fight foreign wars but Parliament had retained the right to collect taxes on the king's behalf. This had been a legacy from a time when courtiers were offered land or titles for supporting the monarch. Charles had become involved in an increasingly expensive war against Spain and although reluctant to do so he had little choice but to ask Parliament for money. Parliament at this time was not a permanent institution, only assembling at the King's request, so following Charles' demands for money, Parliament saw an ideal opportunity to air some of its grievances.

Once Parliament had been assembled, it refused to agree to Charles' demands and offered him one seventh of the money he requested, together with a long list of complaints. Charles was furious and ordered the collection of forced loans; any resistance was met with severe punishment. Parliament, realising that it had angered the king, attempted a reconciliation by proposing a Petition of Rights. Charles immediately dismissed this on the basis that he was supreme ruler over not only the nation, but Parliament as well.

By 1642 this dispute had reached a critical point. Charles desperately needed money but Parliament refused to agree. In desperation Charles marched on Westminster with a band of armed guards, hoping to arrest the ringleaders. On his arrival, Charles found the ringleaders had fled along the River Thames, probably having been forewarned by a sympathiser. Angered, Charles left for the city of Oxford, along with his army and courtiers. Once there he set up an alternative Parliament. With Charles in Oxford and the Westminster Parliament disbanded, England began to fall into state of lawlessness that would eventually lead to civil war.

Oliver Cromwell

Among the parliamentarian supporters, a puritan squire named Oliver Cromwell rose to prominence leading the parliamentarian forces against King Charles' royalist army. Finally in 1645, following a bloody civil war Charles' forces were finally defeated at the Battle of Naseby. What followed was a stalemate with Parliament attempting to negotiate a compromise with the king. After the war Cromwell returned to Cambridge, hoping that a settlement could be reached in his absence. By 1648 Cromwell had lost patience with both the king and the remainder of the Westminster Parliament.

He returned to London and demanded that the king be tried for treason. The juries, handpicked and cajoled by Cromwell's men, were pressed into declaring a guilty verdict. In 1649 Charles I was executed on a scaffold erected in London's Whitehall. With hindsight, if Charles I had been prepared to negotiate with Parliament he might well have survived the crisis. The public certainly had no desire to execute their king and, ultimately, a small group of parliamentarians took the decision on the country's behalf. Following the king's execution, England, Scotland and Wales became a republic for the first and last time (1649 to 1660).

Cromwell 's leadership, however, soon proved to be unpopular with the people. With his puritanical beliefs he put an end to anything he regarded as disrespectful, including festivities, dancing, music and theatre. Following Cromwell's death in 1658, Charles II - son of Charles I - was restored to the throne. Charles II was granted a yearly allowance, which meant he did not have to call Parliament and Parliament was free to convene when it chose to do so. Cromwell, now in disgrace, was disinterred. His head was placed on a spike on the main wall of the Tower of London. And there it remained for twenty years until a gale blew it off!

Revolution in the air

There was an uproar in England in 1801 when England's first

census showed that major cities such as Manchester, Birmingham and Leeds had no representation in Parliament. The philosopher Jeremy Bentham had put forward the people's cause in his book, 'Parliament Reform Catechism,' by arguing for electoral districts. So, encouraged by political radicals and the realisation that the population had little influence over Parliament, 600 petitions were presented to Parliament seeking genuine representation for the people. Parliament dismissed these with contempt, many on the basis that they 'had not taken into account parliamentary procedure.' The public were incensed. France had seen a repressive monarchy guillotined out of existence in 1789 and replaced by a republic, so Parliament was fully aware of what could happen if the public were angered into revolt.

In Britain, although calls for liberty and fraternity were heard, the population became more sanguine, as they experienced rising living standards. Some radicals complained that the British public were more interested in the Prince Regent's marital arrangements, than reforming the class system. Around this time journalism in the form of a 'radical press' and the distribution of free sheets made the public more aware of parliament and encouraged the expectation of greater representation. The majority of people were illiterate, so these free sheets were sometimes read aloud in taverns or coffee shops. We even have an account of Dr Johnson rewriting speeches that MPs had supposedly made, so that his readership could understand them! On the whole, Parliament managed to ignore or dismiss demands for representation, arguing that it rather than the people had the right to make important decisions.

The nineteenth century

The nineteenth century saw the wholesale domination of Westminster by the British aristocracy and landed interests.

Following the agricultural and industrial revolution in England, a small elite class had accumulated vast amounts of wealth. In 1860, with 170 members of Parliament either baronets or sons of peers, Parliament was far from representative. For a time Parliament was referred to as 'Hotel Cecil', as the Prime Minister Lord Salisbury had appointed so many of his relations to ministerial posts! Political parties were also very different. There was no overriding philosophy, except that of accumulating wealth, with many MPs prepared to switch their loyalties on a whim. Westminster was treated by many as a finishing school to hone their social skills before moving into the higher echelons of society.

Parliament was more of an adjudicator between those with moneyed interests in agriculture, mining, railways, shipping and the increasingly rich colonies. In 1883 a survey confirmed people's prejudices, when it was discovered that 'one quarter of England and Wales was owned by a mere 710 citizens'. The public were rarely considered when Parliament proposed legislation (unless it related to taxation). Indeed, it would have been thought eccentric for an MP to propose a bill specifically for the public's benefit.

It was only later, when social reformers such as Lord Shaftesbury proposed legislation on the working conditions of children, that legislation began to be viewed as a tool for social change. Even then the main arguments for change were economic. Until 1893 when Keir Hardie formed the Independent Labour Party, there remained only two major political forces in Britain. The Whigs, also known as the Liberals, and the Conservatives, known as Tories.

Into the twentieth century

Political scandal in Westminster is nothing new but the media's response and the public's perception of government has changed significantly. In 1911 the then Chancellor of the Exchequer Lloyd George was involved in a share trading scandal. He and a second government minister had bought large amounts of shares in the American-owned Marconi Company, knowing that the British government was about to place a huge armaments order. As news broke on the stock market, Marconi shares doubled in value making Lloyd George a fortune overnight.

When he and his colleagues were challenged about their financial acumen, they replied that they had done nothing wrong. By 1916 Lloyd George had become Prime Minister and his compatriot in the affair was made Lord Chief Justice and Viceroy of India! Later, Lloyd George became embroiled in another scandal when it was discovered he was selling honours to raise money for Liberal party funds. Again the newspapers assumed this to be a normal part of Westminster life and for the most part the general public remained unaware of the scandal.

At the turn of the century although women did not play a prominent part in Westminster politics, they were becoming more vocal. Women did not have the right to vote, and they had little financial independence. Yet as far back as 1888, a group of radical women known as the suffragettes had chained themselves to the Common's Public Gallery demanding the right of women to vote. Another group of suffragettes sailed along the River Thames and moored a boat on to Westminster's Commons Terrace, shouting political slogans through the library window. Despite their voluble protests, the majority of MPs were adamant that women should not be given the right to vote.

Expediency rather than fairness was to become the eventual catalyst for change. The First World War 1914-18 clarified the obvious. If women were able to work in armaments' factories, mine coal, and harvest fields, then they could be trusted with a vote. Despite fierce opposition, in 1917 women over the age of thirty were given the right to vote. *Again, what we see is not a government reacting to the needs of more than half of its population, but a pragmatic response to necessity.* There had been so many men killed or injured during the First World War that it became imperative that women should be given more opportunity if Britain was to recover economically.

The thirties and forties

In the early nineteen thirties, Winston Churchill was considered by some in his own Conservative Party to be a brilliant maverick and by others a liability. At one point, Churchill crossed the floor of the House of Commons to join Lloyd George's Liberal Party, describing the Tories as 'a party of great vested interests, bonded together in a formidable confederation, corruption at home, aggression to cover it up abroad.'[1] This withering attack did not deter Churchill from rejoining the Conservatives in 1924. Churchill, who had been an army officer and a journalist, was to become a lone voice in Parliament, warning against the threat of German rearmament. Dismissed as fanciful by many, his pleadings were largely ignored. Until in 1939 Hitler seized control of Austria, then went on to invade the Sudeten Lands.

Britain and her Commonwealth allies stood alone against a Nazi-Soviet pact until 1943 when the United States of America entered the war. Germany eventually turned against Russia and the tide of war gradually turned in the allies' favour. By August 1945 the allies had been victorious. Britain had won a moral victory but had been financially bankrupt by the cost of the war. What is often overlooked is that if Britain had been overrun Britain, as was expected in 1940, Germany may well have gone on to develop transatlantic nuclear missiles ahead of the Americans. Britain had access to considerable scientific knowledge and the course of modern democracy might have been very different.

The fifties and sixties

The fifties was a period of great shortage but the British economy had started to show some small signs of recovery. In 1956 a dramatic twist in world events was to have serious repercussions for both Britain and France. Egyptian leader Colonel Abdel Nasser nationalised the Suez Canal, a strategically and economically important route in the Middle East. Although British Prime Minister Anthony Eden had agreed with the French that the canal needed to be brought back under their control, they failed to discuss this with their other allies. A military operation was mounted but despite its success the plan backfired when both the Americans and the United Nations refused their financial or political support. Political pressure from the embarrassing disaster forced Eden to resign.

In 1962 Fidel Castro had offered to place Russian missiles on Cuban soil. Not surprisingly the Americans, alarmed at the prospect of nuclear missiles within striking range of their major cities, threatened military action and instigated a naval blockade. At the last moment Russia backed down and dismantled the missiles. Some years later, when secret documents of the period were declassified, it became clear how close the world had come to nuclear war. By the end of 1963, President J. F. Kennedy had been assassinated while travelling in a motorcade in Ohio and the American people were left to mourn the loss of a leader who had taken them through a particularly difficult period of the Cold War.

Meanwhile, in 1963 Westminster was to become embroiled in a sex scandal. Undercover journalists had been tipped off that John

Profumo, the Minister for War, was conducting an adulterous relationship with a young prostitute called Christine Keeler. Less attention would have been paid to this, except that she was also involved with a senior Russian Diplomat called Captain Ivanov. Played out against the Cold War, this had potentially enormous security implications. Profumo was eventually sacked, for repeatedly lying to Parliament - the public was not made aware of the full story for another forty years.

The sixties and seventies

Harold Wilson arrived at Downing Street in 1964, hoping to usher in a period of industrial calm. London heralded an era of cultural freedom and Carnaby Street became home to the Swinging Sixties. Britain was a trendy place to be. However, this did little for industrial relations, as Britain went from one economic crisis to another. Through Wilson, Heath, Wilson again and then Callaghan, the electorate no sooner adjusted to one government than it was presented with another. While the United States managed to send its umpteenth man to the moon, Britain was enjoying the Victorian revival of candlelight through the 1978 Winter of Discontent. The Trade Unions were plied with sandwiches and bottles of beer at Downing Street, while the British public sat back and wondered.

British industrial relations over this period were dreadful and the combination of greedy bosses and militant unions, controlling Britain's essential services, meant that Britain suffered a period of relative economic decline. As usual it was the public who had to endure the consequences as Japan, Hong Kong and Taiwan raced ahead with their increasingly modern and efficient industries. So when in 1970, Edward Heath was elected Prime Minister the Common Market seemed like a shortcut to affluence. The problem was that no matter how appealing the Common Market looked, Britain was still not producing enough high-quality goods that other nations wanted to buy. Britain was soon suffering a three-day working week, 20 per cent inflation and a worsening economy.[2]

Scandal was to hit Westminster again in 1972, when the businessman John Poulson was discovered paying MPs, civil servants, local councillors, council officials and NHS employees, large amounts of cash to secure government contracts. This only came to light after Poulson's architectural business filled for bankruptcy in February 1972 at Wakefield Crown Court. As a result, he and some of his colleagues were jailed and tighter regulations controlling local council budgets were introduced although the actual convictions were widely regarded as the tip of the iceberg to an extensive network of corruption.

Thatcherism

Although Mrs Thatcher had first entered Parliament in 1959, it wasn't until 1979 that she won the parliamentary seat of East Finchley and became the UK's first women Prime Minister. The Rubicon had been crossed. As Mrs Thatcher wryly said, 'I did not get here by being stridently female.'[3] as much a comment on Westminster's male dominated character as her own determination. Not since Nancy Astor had become the first woman MP in 1919 had a woman achieved such a prominent position in Parliament. Many of Mrs Thatcher's colleagues, who were anticipating a casual saunter through the autumn term, were rudely awakened.

Mrs Thatcher's eleven years in office saw a profound change in British society and a dramatic shift towards a market-driven economy. Her premiership witnessed Britain go to war against Argentina over the Falkland Islands in 1982, and the collapse of the Berlin

Wall in 1989, marking the end of the Cold War. What is often forgotten is that Mrs Thatcher's fall from grace was not from losing a general election. She did something far worse - she lost the confidence of her trusted political colleagues. Although her policies divided the nation, one issue lay at the heart of British democracy. Should the Conservative Party have been able to remove one Prime Minister and replace her with another, without seeking the views of the electorate? As Parliament began to behave more like the Roman Senate, the British public felt a growing detachment from their elected representatives.

Conclusions

As you can see, the development of democracy has mainly been driven by crisis and pragmatism. The electorate have only ever been given limited rights, as power was transferred away from powerful interest groups. *Representative democracy did not evolve from a desire to represent all the electorate but from the influence of smaller pressure groups.* Indeed, all of the major political parties have their origins in representing interested groups of one form or another. The Tories supported landowners, the Liberals the aristocracy, and Labour the trade unions.

We might enjoy the benefits of some legislation but we still have to live with their political paymasters. Even the most popular governments have reflected their political origins. Henry Campbell-Bannerman in 1908 laid the foundations for the Welfare State, after pressure from left-wing radicals. McCawley repealed the Corn Laws in 1902, with an eye to supporting wealthy landowners. Governments being influenced by financial paymasters is nothing new, but the idea that the public should have a say in what government can and cannot do certainly is. *Direct democracy is the first democratic movement specifically formed to represent the whole of the electorate.*

SECTION THREE

Grumpy Dumpty

Grumpy Dumpty sat on the floor
Grumpy Dumpty was a big bore
He never said thankyou
He never said please
So they scrambled his brain
And ate it for tea

Chapter Five

✔

The Missing Constitution

As with many things in the United Kingdom, the lack of a definitive constitution appears to many outsiders as an anomaly. The UK is an active member of a variety of international bodies, yet retains a strong national identity. It has areas of relative deprivation, yet is still one of the richest nations in the world.[1] It has a constitution that it is largely unwritten, based on precedent and adapted in a politically pragmatic fashion, which has come about mainly due to a series of historical quirks. Although some of the UK's statute laws are treated as constitutional law, many are based on convention and are vulnerable to interpretation.

The Crown, Parliament, the Civil Service and the Judiciary are all outward signs of this constitution but the UK has not had a comprehensive constitutional document since the Bill of Rights Act in 1689. Today the UK, New Zealand and Israel are alone in not having a definitive written constitution to represent the rights and responsibilities of the people. The danger is that freedoms so dearly bought are being lost.

Traditionally British 'citizens' have enjoyed the freedom to do whatever they want, as long as it is not unlawful. This is subtly different to many countries where citizens have inalienable rights to do thing anything that is legal. In Britain this has produced a tolerant and considerate society but it relies on three important factors:

- First, a mutual consideration for others. For instance, in the UK you would be at liberty to stand on a street corner with a sign on your head saying: 'I Love Santa Clause - He Brought Me Some Great Presents.' As long as you didn't harm anyone else you could stand there all day. In many other countries you would be quickly moved on or arrested. The problem is that these freedoms are worthless unless citizens are prepared to show due consideration to others. The same good manners, courtesy and patience that the British are renowned for, are under severe strain from a small proportion of the population, who consider their recidivist behaviour acceptable. The UK's liberal notion of democracy has created a vacuum that some are intent upon abusing. If one person jumps the queue, soon everybody has to jump the queue, just to stay in line.

- Secondly, this type of democracy relies on the government's ability to make decisions without interference from external sovereign bodies. This could be described as a nation's sovereign right to act. Yet the wishes of the British public have not kept pace with the ambitions of some politicians.

  The rise of international institutions such as the EU, the United Nations, the World Bank, the International Monetary Fund, the World Trade Organisation and NATO have all diminished the sovereignty of Westminster's Parliament. This is not to say that all of these international bodies are inherently bad but we can legitimately ask, who are they supposed to represent?

- Third, in a society that relies on freedoms, rather than 'rights', the public are given no option but to trust their elected representatives. As Lord Mackay stated:

> 'In the absence of a written constitution in the conventional sense, we place considerable weight on practice and convention. The judgement, discretion and good faith of those operating our constitutional arrangements is of the greatest importance. It is a strength rather than a weakness. It inculcates mutual recognition and understanding of the respective roles and permits flexibility and adaptation to developing circumstance. As long as the people in public life with the necessary qualities - and I believe that we are very fortunate in this respect - I think our arrangements work at least as well, perhaps better than many others.'[2]

This are fine words from a Lord Chancellor with a reputation for integrity but can we trust politicians, to always act with such high values? As L. S. Amery once said of British democracy, it is 'one of democracy but of democracy by consent and not by delegation, of government of the people, for the people, with but not by the people.'[3] This would seem on the face of a polite way of telling the electorate to keep out of what is being done on their behalf.

Checks on the abuse of power

In theory, the UK has three basic principles that are a check on the abuse of power by government or external international bodies. These could be described as the sovereignty of Parliament, the separation of powers and the rule of law. The idea being that not all power is concentrated in the hands of a few individuals. The problem is that the British government now controls both the legislature (courts) and the executive (government) and it has the right to give itself as much power as it chooses, without having to consult parliament with the use of it's prerogative powers.

As Anthony Barnett points out, 'in Britain the powers of government are not clearly separated; the executive (government) is unchecked; nor since joining Europe, is Parliament supreme; and internationally established rights cannot possibly sit comfortably with the UK's constitution.'[4] The European Union has further weakened the UK's sovereignty, despite assurances by successive governments. As Philip Norton points out, 'legislation emanating from the European Communities was deemed to have precedence over legislation passed by the Westminster Parliament.'[5] Ironically, although unrepresentative, the House of Lords did put a check on the excesses of the executive. But even here there has been an attempt to fill the House of Lords with peers who are more compliant with New Labour's wishes.

The prerogative powers of government

The government has relinquished many areas of British sovereignty by using a legal process called the Crown Prerogative. This could more accurately be described as the Government Prerogative. Albert Venn Dicey described the prerogative as the 'residue of discretionary or arbitrary authority, which at any time is legally left in the hands of the Crown.'[6] It is either a major constitutional failing or an efficient means of governing, depending on whether or not you are the holder of its power. Its origins lay in a time when monarchs ruled with absolute power, believing themselves to be above everyone, except God. The prerogative entitled them to: recognise foreign states; enter into national treaties; enter into diplomatic relations; control the armed forces; direct intelligence services; declare war; rally troops; or declare peace.

When Parliament appropriated the powers of Charles I, it took the power of the Royal Prerogative for itself. The prerogative could be described as every act that can be done lawfully by the executive government without needing the authority of Parliament. When Parliament is dissolved prior to a general election it uses its prerogative powers. When a bill passes from the House of Commons to the

House of Lords to become law the prerogative is again sighted. The appointment of a prime minister, the appointment of judges, ambassadors, the granting of honours, the regulation of the civil service, the raising and spending of taxes, the pardoning of offenders or the use of nolle prosequi (where a criminal prosecution can be halted by government). Even the appointment of the director general of the BBC is made under the government's prerogative.

The prerogative – use or misuse?

Some prerogative powers are essential if governments are to act speedily. An example was in 1982, when Mrs Thatcher dispatched a military task force to the South Atlantic, several days prior to a debate in the House of Commons, in anticipation of the Falklands Conflict. As the Argentinians had already invaded the islands, it would have seemed churlish to have a debate about when troops might be dispatched. Problems arise though, when these prerogative powers are abused. In 1992 with a much-reduced parliamentary majority, John Major threatened to use the prerogative against Parliament, if it did not ratify the Maastricht European Treaty. *In effect, John Major held Parliament to ransom over what was an important constitutional question that should have been put to the electorate.* More recently Tony Blair used the prerogative to confer special status on Jonathan Powell, as Chief of Staff, and Alastair Campbell, as Chief Press Secretary, allowing them to instruct civil servants.

The fact that the government possesses a legal device to force through legislation, make public appointments, raise unlimited amounts of taxes, spend this on what it wants, give as much sovereignty away as it chooses and increase its own power without consultation is clearly absurd in a modern democracy. Obviously, no government has any interest in amending what is in effect a means to govern without accountability. As the UK does not have a clearly defined constitution, it goes some way towards explaining why so much authority has been passed to international bodies without consulting the British electorate. In recent years, the British government has given control of its trade laws, immigration policy, fishing rights, prison sentencing, international law, human rights legislation and now asylum law, to a variety of international bodies who supersede the authority of the UK's Parliament.

By the people for the people

Clearly, the UK does not have an adequate means of checking the abuse of power by a determined government. In fact:

> 'the one source [of power] is now mainly embodied in the Prime Minister, who has appropriated almost all the royal prerogatives... In fact, if not in theory the Prime Minister is Head of State, Chief Executive and Chief Legislator and while in office is not circumscribed by any clear or binding constitutional limitations. Again in Britain there is not a single alternative source of secure constitutional power at any level.'[7]

So what checks are left against tyranny? There is an election every five years, although a governing party could attempt to change this. There are opposition parties but they are less and less effective. Lastly, the UK's Head of State, Queen Elizabeth II, could theoretically refuse to recognise a government. *Ultimately as more power has been concentrated in fewer and fewer hands, the public has little option but to rely on the good intentions of politicians!*

The UK needs a written constitution that would clearly set out the responsibilities of government and the relationship between government and its citizens. Indeed Mr Blair himself said in 1994 that the UK needs 'a new constitutional settlement to express the new relationship between individual and society, citizen and state, for the world today.'[8] Even the Chancellor Gordon Brown is on record as saying that:

> 'Britain needs a modern constitution and a modern view of the rule of government. The challenge of the 1990s is to create a settlement that recognises both our rights and aspirations as individuals and our needs and shared values as a community,'

- after he summarised Charter 88's campaign for a written constitution.

What is required is a written constitution that sets out legal boundaries at national, regional and local level. *This would become the authoritative text on what powers the government holds and would highlight the responsibilities of:* the Head of State; the Executive; elected and appointed politicians; the legislatures; regional government; the judiciary; public services (responsibility to citizens); the armed forces; police; and the intelligence services.

A written Constitution

A constitution might also contain a Bill of Rights containing a set of principles of general consensus. The government prerogative would be clearly limited. For example no international agreements could be entered into without the consent of the majority of the electorate in a referendum and no amendments could be made to the constitution without recourse to the electorate.

It might contain a concise definition of the public's freedom of expression and constitute an acceptable definition of free speech and language, rather than hiding behind a politically motivated definition of 'correctness'.

So, to summarise, a written constitution might contain at least the following points. It would:

- become the sole foundation for the executive, legislature and judicial powers.

- confirm that the position of the Head of State is held by Queen Elizabeth II, her successor and heirs.

- state that the executive government is restrained by conditions contained within the constitution.

- define the governing executive as containing the Prime Minister, ministers of government and MPs.

- recognise the inalienable rights of its citizens, such as the freedom from illegal imprisonment (unless the law had been broken), the confiscation of property; and freedom from persecution.

- would set out both the rights and responsibilities of citizens and governments.

- confirm the right of all citizens to vote in elections (or not to vote).

- only apply to nationals and not be extended to non-nationals.

- give the public the right of access to information held by public authorities. (Subject to limitations over national security concerns, the legal enforcement of the law and the prevention of terrorism).

- take out of the hands of politicians, the appointment of the judiciary (to be given to a completely independent body that is elected by the electorate for a term of ten years).

- legitimise the right of abode in the United Kingdom for any citizen holding British nationality.

- regulate the armed forces together with the territorial and reserve military forces through acts of Parliament.

- uphold the freedom to participate and initiate proposals and referendums, the results of which would be binding to the government and its citizens, subject to certain exceptions (such as defence and national security).

So has anyone ever attempted to write such a constitution? In 1991 the Institute for Public Policy Research published a book called 'The Constitution of Britain',[9] which is a comprehensive document that gives us some idea of how a written constitution might be set out.

Conclusion

In conclusion, the most compelling argument for a written constitution is to protect the citizens of any nation from its own elected representatives. As Simon Jenkins points out:

> 'As long as Britain has no written constitution and concentrates all governmental power in the hands of a few of the leadership of a Commons majority, that leadership will always seek more.'[10]

The argument for any democracy to have a definitive constitution is overwhelming. For those countries that already have written constitutions it would be a relatively straightforward procedure to include an article defining the rights of citizens to vote on questions of government policy. For nations that have experienced representative democracy for some years, the only obstruction to the introduction of direct democracy is from politicians who are reluctant to relinquish their own power.

As E. H. Carr wrote, 'the past is intelligible to us only in the light of the present; and we can fully understand the present only in the light of the past'.[11] We do not have to live in the past but a better understanding of our history gives us more control over our future. Representative democracy should be seen as a step towards an accountable executive, within a framework of direct democracy.

Chapter Six

✔

The Rise of the Nation State

Although the description 'Britain' or the 'United Kingdom' appear interchangeable, in the strictest sense, Britain could be thought of as 'three identifiable national units,' comprising of Scotland, England and Wales. When Northern Ireland is included, the region is usually referred to as the United Kingdom of Great Britain and Northern Ireland. However the definition of the British Isles would also include islands such as the Shetlands, Orkney, Isle of Man, Jersey and Guernsey, which all have a degree of political autonomy from Westminster (with clearly defined security and trading arrangements with the UK).

More than most nations, the UK's political development has been closely tied up with its monarchy. Of course if we travel back in time we can see that Britain was not an integrated state but a collection of various warring tribes that were gradually brought together under external threat. Britain has only been conquered and settled in twice, first by the Romans then by William of Normandy. Even then, Scotland remained for the most part free of Roman rule. Once the Romans had suppressed the various indigenous tribes, they quickly went about introducing Roman law and taxation.

By the fourth century Rome had converted to the new religion of Christianity and although not widely accepted in Britain until a century later, British culture and laws were greatly affected by these ancient influences. By the eighth century Britain was separated into areas dominated by groups such as the Ancient Britons, Saxons, Angles, Celts and the Jutes. With increasingly ferocious attacks from Norwegian, Danish and Swedish Norsemen, the Anglo-Saxons were forced back into a small area in Wessex (Hampshire, Wiltshire and Somerset), but in 878 AD the Anglo-Saxon King Alfred decisively defeated the Danish invaders and Britain began to enjoy a period of relative calm.

William of Normandy

In 1066 William arrived from Normandy and defeated King Harold just outside the small Sussex town of Battle close to Hastings. Harold had anticipated a Norman attack but while waiting for the Normans, he was informed of another attack by the Norwegian king, Harald Hardrada. Harold had little choice but to force his army to march over 200 miles to Stamford Bridge near York. Here he defeated Hardrada's forces in a ferocious battle, before turning South towards Sussex, only to be told that the Normans had already landed in Sussex.

Harold was defeated at what became known as the Battle of Hastings and William of Normandy became King of England conferring on himself the title of William the Conqueror. William's reign was marked by violence and brutality. Ambitious to unite England under his rule, William set about cataloguing the lands that were now under his authority. This was to become known as the Doomsday Book, a means to raise political, financial and military support for William.

Henry II

It is during the reign of Henry II (1154-89) that we see the first signs of a unified English state and the introduction of a common legal system. The king's responsibility was to administer the nation and, when called upon, to defend its borders from invasion. When Henry needed to raise money or men, he would sell peerages and honours to those who controlled his lands. This was not only an effective way of raising revenue, it guaranteed a loyalty from his nobles. It was also to become the basis of Britain's peculiar class system for the next two thousand years. The king's most trusted supporters were collectively known as the Kings Council (later the Privy Council) and his immediate advisers were known as the cabinet.

This extension of decision-making was the first step towards representative democracy, with the King's House of Lords containing the King's Parliament. The king's unlimited power was, in practice, limited by the support of his Lords. During King John's time on the throne, a dispute arose that would lead to an early constitutional crisis. Complaints were made about the amount of taxation, restrictions on travel and the means by which the Criminal Justice system was being implemented. This was to be resolved with the signing of the Magna Carta document at Runnymede in 1215. It is also where Britain derives its right to trial by jury and the king's acknowledgement that the legal process alone can determine someone's guilt or innocence.

By the thirteenth century we can see the origins of Parliament's House of Commons. Edward I would, at his discretion, summon representatives from the English counties and boroughs to bring their disagreements to Parliament in the form of petitions. At Westminster today, a baize bag still hangs behind the Speaker's chair, which still contains receipts for the day's petitions. This petitioning became immensely popular, not least because prior to this arrangement arguments were frequently settled with duels! By the time Edward III was king, the House of Commons had became well established but it was not until much later that Parliament would meet on a regular basis.

Henry VII and Henry VIII

In 1171 the Catholic Pope Adrian IV had conferred on Henry II the overlordship of Ireland. This status was intended for the purpose of reforming incalcitrant members of the Irish Church. Later, after Henry VIII broke with Rome over his marital problems, some of the Irish called on Rome and Spain for their support in defeating the now Protestant English. In 1541 Henry brutally crushed the Irish rebellion and by 1541 the Irish Parliament was forced to recognise Henry as ruler of Ireland. After Henry's death, he was succeeded by his brilliant but ailing son Edward VI, who tragically died at the age of sixteen.

Henry's daughter Mary, a devout Catholic, succeeded Edward. Under Henry and Edward the trappings of Catholicism had been repressed but Mary's rule (1553-58) Catholicism was reintroduced together with the full-scale persecution of Protestants throughout England. Mary's five-year reign saw hundreds of Protestants martyred in a bloody drive to stamp out Protestantism. The common people never forgave her and associated Catholicism with oppression and violence. Mary died at the age of forty-one and was succeeded by her sister Elizabeth I who was to reign from 1558 to 1603.

Elizabeth I – the 'Virgin Queen'

Elizabeth, a devout Protestant, required her people to publicly comply with the Protestant religion but was generally tolerant of Catholic practises (if kept within the home). She was aware of what had occurred under Mary's rule and recognised that the country needed a period of stability. In affairs of state and trade Elizabeth proved to be a consummate diplomat. By the end of her reign the cultural arts in Britain were flourishing with theatre, poetry and drama becoming immensely popular. Marlowe, Shakespeare and Johnson were all popular across the whole range of social classes. Elizabeth was respected and loved by her people and feared by her enemies. Adventures such as Sir Francis Drake's Voyage of Discovery and the destruction of the Spanish Armada in 1858 only added to her mystic and power.

Elizabeth I had managed to achieve what seemed like a contradiction. She had laid the foundations for a tolerant society, where art and literature were to flourish, while making England one of the most powerful nations in the world. By 1603 James VI of Scotland had become James I of England, uniting the crowns of both the Scottish and England. Unfortunately, James did not inherit Elizabeth's financial sense. Within two years his extravagant lifestyle and a lavish court had increased the country's balance of payments deficit, to over half a million pounds. A truly vast sum of money at that time. James did not prove to be particularly popular, although he was shrewd enough to be cautious in his dealings with Parliament.

Charles I

Charles I came to the throne in 1625 and could not have been more unlike his father James in character. He was pious, reflective and serious with little time for the bawdy behaviour that had been common in James' court. Charles' unwillingness to compromise with Parliament was eventually to cost him the English throne and his life. By 1645 Charles had decisively lost against the parliamentarian forces led by Oliver Cromwell and he fled to Scotland. The Scots never having forgiven Charles for the introduction of the

English prayer book, refused him safe refuge and handed him back to the parliamentary forces. Charles was executed in 1649 in London.

By the time Charles I's son, Charles II, was reinstated to the throne, he was to oversee a cultural and economic renaissance that saw literature, science, theatre, medicine, exploration, astronomy and trade prosper. With figures such as Sir Isaac Newton and Descartes publishing their theories on science and philosophy, people everywhere began to re-access the way they viewed the world. In Westminster, after the chaos of the civil war, there emerged a loose affiliation of political groups. These were not so much distinct political parties, but small groups linked together by common allegiances.

James II, William and Ireland

By the mid-1680s James II had attempted to reintroduce a Catholic monarchy and political reforms to Britain by secretly enlisting his Catholic allies France and Spain. Eventually James' forces were routed by soldiers loyal to Parliament and James was forced to flee to France. King William and Mary of Holland were invited by Parliament to become Britain's new monarchy, but aware of the risks, Parliament set out a monarch's rights and responsibilities in the 1689 Bill of Rights Act.

What we see is a document that limits the power of the monarchy, without fundamentally undermining the Royal Prerogative. At the same time it restricted any resurgence of political Catholicism. By 1690 William and Mary were under threat from the French. James II had devised a Jacobean plot to assassinate William and restore himself to the throne. In Ireland James raised an army and attempted to subdue the Protestants in the North. William, a staunch protestant, led an army against James' forces and defeated him at the Battle of the Boyne in July 1690. The repercussions of this would last for many years with the troubles in Ireland.

Up until the 1700s, the relationship between Scotland and England was characterised by intermittent conflict. Both the Scottish and the English began to realise that some sort of treaty had to be agreed upon. By the time Queen Anne came to the throne in 1703, she encouraged her English government to seek a Treaty with Scotland, which came into effect in May 1707. Central to the treaty was that Scotland's Presbyterian faith and separate legal system were to continue. The effect of this was to abolish the Scottish Parliament (until recent devolution) and incorporate Scottish MPs into Westminster.

There were benefits for both England and Scotland. Primarily for Scotland the advantages were economic, as Scotland had been denied access to England's lucrative colonial markets. England gained peace with her neighbour for the first time in hundreds of years. Both countries gained in the transfer of academic, industrial and agricultural skills that were to have enormous benefits during the industrial revolution. Many Scots began to settle in England and many English businesses established offices in Scotland.

George II

By George II's reign we begin to see what we would recognise as the modern Parliament of Westminster. Although Parliament could propose and debate legislation, the king still had significant powers giving Royal Consent to all acts of Parliament. In 1745 Charles Edward Stuart (Bonnie Prince Charlie), the grandson of James II, attempted to regain power during a Jacobite uprising. Fighting against the Parliamentary forces he managed to capture Edinburgh, Carlisle and Derby before being defeated by forces loyal to King George at the Battle of Culloden in 1746.

By 1793 France had declared war on Britain and her ally Holland. Invasion seemed imminent and the upper classes watched in horror as the French revolution claimed more and more victims. By 1805 Nelson had crushed the French and Spanish fleet at the Battle of Trafalgar and the Duke of Wellington had defeated Napoleon in 1815 at the Battle of Waterloo. Britain emerged from the French Napoleonic wars with the largest military force that the world had ever seen. Despite the victory, British soldiers were returning home to poverty, hardship and repression. In a wave of popular anger, a group called the Luddites set about destroying industrial and agricultural machinery that seemed to threaten their prospects of finding employment.

Around this time, the political philosopher Thomas Paine had proposed that individuals had inherent rights that government should not be allowed to ignore. With Paine's idea of universal male suffrage becoming more widely accepted, demands were made for the reform of the British electoral system. In 1819 a political meeting in Manchester was dispersed with such violence, that eleven rioters were killed. This was to become known as the Peterloo Massacre. Faced with increasing calls for the recognition of workers rights, the government responded by executing many of the ringleaders.

The Reform Act of 1832

When George III died in 1820 he was succeeded by his eldest son George IV, who reigned for ten years until William IV took the throne. Although William's reign was only to last seven years, it was to see momentous parliamentary changes. By 1828 the radical Francis Place had drafted a people's charter, proposing the vote for eligible men, the abolition of property qualifications, salaries for Members of Parliament (so that being an MP was not dependent on a private income), secret ballots and annual Parliaments.

Any idea that the public should be represented in Parliament was considered revolutionary.

Representation in Parliament at this time relied on a corrupt system of boroughs, each being entitled to send representatives to Westminster. But these boroughs were still controlled by a small group of gentry and landowners. The most notorious example was Old Sarum that was represented by two Westminster MPs even though it only had seven constituents! Eventually, the Reform Act of 1832 was passed, despite strong opposition from the Tories in the House of Lords. The bill was eventually passed when after a general election the king threatened to create new Lords who would be sympathetic to the bill.

During the reign of Queen Victoria from 1837, Britain was at the height of its international power. Although Victoria was not involved in the day-to-day running of Parliament, she did appoint Prime Ministers and still had to consent to any parliamentary legislation. For the general public any entitlement to vote was still regarded as a privilege, as it depended upon owning property, paying enough rent or earning a level of wages that were beyond the means of most people. Three out of five men and all women were still barred from voting. Tying the 'privilege' of voting to income had the effect of it becoming a goal that the middle classes would aspire to and would eventually lead to universal representation. Queen Victoria was to die in 1901, to be succeeded by King Edward VII. George V was to inherit the throne in 1910, followed by King Edward VIII in 1936.

Chapter Seven

Elizabeth II

The abdication of Edward VIII was to have profound consequences on a little girl called Elizabeth, who at that time was living with her parents in Bruton Street, Mayfair, London. Edward had fallen in love with the American divorcee Mrs Wallis Warfield Simpson. The dilemma for the king was that in Britain in 1936 it was considered unconstitutional for a monarch to marry a divorcee. Both the Canadian and American newspapers had been printing rumours about the relationship for months but in Britain the press had been more restrained.

On Thursday 10 December 1936, following a farewell dinner with his family and close friends, King Edward VIII broadcast his final speech as king to a bewildered nation;

'I have found it impossible to carry the heavy burden of responsi-
· bility and to discharge my duties as King as I would wish to do
without the help and support of the woman I love.'

The next day at 1.52pm, Friday 11 December 1936, King George VI, Edward's brother was formally pronounced King of Great Britain, Ireland and the Dominions beyond the seas. Elizabeth II and her sister Margaret were to become known as the young princesses. Edward VIII from this time on would take the title of the Duke of Windsor.

The prospect of war

In March 1936 while Edward VIII was still king, the German army had marched into the Rhineland, despite treaties that had existed since the end of the First World War. Germany had secretly signed treaties with both Italy and Japan while actively supporting the Fascists in the Spanish civil war. Britain's government at the time was essentially a coalition of various political parties. In 1938 Chamberlain went to Munich to meet with senior Nazi leaders. He returned with what was to become the infamous agreement that was supposedly going to bring 'peace in our time'. By 22 August 1939, news broke that Germany had signed a Nazi-Soviet pact and by September Britain was at war.

In the first year of the war Britain had little to celebrate. On 14 October 1939 a German submarine infiltrated the Royal Navy's defences at Scapa Flow and sunk the battleship Royal Oak, with the loss of 880 lives. By 9 April 1940, German forces had occupied Denmark and attacked Norway. British and Canadian Expeditionary forces that had been sent to protect Norway were overwhelmed. In Parliament on 8 February 1940, the Conservatives and a number of opposition MPs joined forces to defeat the coalition government. Chamberlain offered his resignation to the king.

Winston Churchill

Few people wanted the job of a Prime Minister who would be leading the country to war against a revitalised Germany. Churchill, who had been warning of the Nazi threat for five years, was asked by the king if he would head the government. News about the progress of the war did not improve. By 31 May British troops who were able to make their way to Dunkirk in France were evacuated. Although the rescue was miraculous, it was obvious to most people that Britain was now in desperate straits. Churchill was aware from intelligence reports that Hitler intended to invade Britain on 1 August 1940, once Goering's Luftwaffe had destroyed the Royal Air Force.

Evacuation

Throughout Europe, prominent people with influence became a target for Nazi attention. In Norway and Holland the Nazi's attempted to capture the Royal families. In London plans were made to evacuate Princess Elizabeth and Margaret to Canada but eventually the king and Churchill decided that it was more important that the family stay together, at least until it became clear what dangers they faced. If the Nazis had managed to capture the British Royal family, it would have been an enormous propaganda coup. Churchill was also aware that an abortive attempt to kidnap the Duke of Windsor had been planned, while the Duke was in Lisbon en route to take up a post as the governor of the Bahamas.

By September 1940 bombing raids were becoming more frequent across London and although the East End and the London Docks took most of the punishment, Buckingham Palace and the Houses of Parliament were also targeted. On 13 September after repeated attempts by the Luftwaffe, a German bomber came close to killing both the king and Princess Elizabeth. Elizabeth wrote in her diary:

> 'the King and I saw two of the bombs quite close to us in the quadrangle. They screamed past the window and exploded with a tremendous boom and crash about fifteen yards away.'[1]

Despite the damage caused, these attacks had the effect of producing a sense of solidarity between the royal family and the nation. The war was to last until April 1945 but postwar, Britain and the Empire had been changed irrevocably. By the time the king had departed for his tour of South African in 1947, it was obvious to the public that he was desperately ill. In January 1948 he was diagnosed with arteriosclerosis due to smoking and eventually died on 6 February 1952, at the age of fifty-six.

Princess Elizabeth's coronation was the first to be televised, although there were misgivings about the idea. With encouragement from Churchill, it was decided that the broadcast should go ahead. On 2 June 1953 at 12.00am the world watched as Princess Elizabeth spoke her coronation oath and became Queen Elizabeth II. Westminster Abbey's choir sang Handel's 'Zadok the Priest' and an estimated 27 million people in Britain alone watched or listened to the coronation via the BBC.[2] In later years the Queen would talk about the events:

> 'In a way I didn't have an apprenticeship, my father died much too young - It was all very sudden, just taking on and making the best job you can. It's a question of just maturing into what you're doing and accepting that here you are and it's your fate. I think continuity is very important. It is a job for life.'[3]

Elizabeth's reign has seen enormous changes in Britain and around the world. There are few politicians who could claim to have such a breadth of experience of world events including: Indian Independence; the Berlin Airlift; the Korean War; the Suez Crisis; the Cold War; the Falklands War; the return of Hong Kong to China, September 11 and two Gulf Wars.

A constitutional monarch

At first sight, the power of Britain's constitutional Head of State appears ceremonial but in strict legal terms her responsibilities are extensive. The pomp and ceremony that tourists see is only the outward sign of duties that go largely unnoticed. For example if a government attempted to extend its term of office to an unlimited period, the Queen would be within her rights to dissolve Parliament. Or if a group attempted a military coup, as happened in Spain in 1976, the Queen would be able to call upon both the armed forces and the police in the legitimate defence of the country.

In practice many of the Queen's rights are waived, such as refusing to sign a parliamentary bill or appointing a Prime Minister of her own choosing. You might think these powers have never been used but for a short period in 1957 Britain was without a Prime Minister. The Conservative Anthony Eden had resigned due to ill health and the Queen, after considering the advice of her ministers appointed Harold Macmillan. Even today in the event of a 'hung Parliament' it would be at the Queen's discretion to appoint a new Prime Minister or advise on a general election. *The essence of a constitutional monarch is that the monarch remains politically impartial but is available to offer ministers advice.*

It is up to her ministers whether or not they take notice. As Bagehot pointed out, 'The importance of the monarchy, lies not in its power but in its influence.' Having reigned for over fifty years and having worked with ten Prime Ministers, Elizabeth, as acting Head of State, 'has the right to be consulted, the right to encourage and the right to warn'.[4] She also plays a key role in supporting British overseas interests. Although in recent years, what we have witnessed is a rather *impetuous* government acting without the usual consultation. As was pointed out in 1997 following the visit of the American president, 'it was an extraordinary lack of courtesy that no one bothered to pick up the phone and ask her, whether she would like to meet the President to come to see her privately.'[5]

The Queen is also head of the fifty-four Commonwealth countries that have a combined population of nearly 2 billion people.[6]

In the past she has been involved in a variety of trade and political agreements, having the advantage of established diplomatic relationships with many other world leaders. The stability and continuance of the monarchy, compared to the transience of politicians does seem to contribute to the smooth running of the country. Moreover the UK's constitutional monarch has become an important part of the nation's national identity.

The Privy Council

The Queen's Privy Council is the means by which the Queen is able to advise her government on matters of state and diplomacy. The council consists of one half peers and the other half commoners who meet with the Queen on a regular basis. Subjects might include thoughts that the Queen has over legislation or the enactment of bills. Occasionally a Privy Council might hold an emergency meeting, such as in 1998 when a question arose as to whether the Lockerbie trial could take place in the Netherlands. A Privy Council meeting was set up in the VIP lounge at Heathrow. The council also has various duties relating to organisations that are under the Royal Charter, such as the General Medical Council and the Royal College of Veterinary Surgeons.

So what does being the British Head of State entail? The Queen's day would normally start around 7am with a review of the daily newspapers over breakfast. She might then read a selection of the 200 to 300 letters she receives every day, with the remaining letters being answered by her private secretaries. After breakfast the Queen and her senior private secretary would go through boxes of official government papers and accounts which have been sent from ministers or representatives of the Commonwealth. They would cover a wide range of subjects, such as the Dissolution of Parliament or the confirmation of Bank Holidays. Around mid-morning she would hold a series of audiences with foreign ambassadors, senior civil servants, members of the armed forces, church leaders and judges.

With audiences lasting between ten and twenty minutes, this would take up much of the morning. It would normally end with a meeting of her Privy Council advisors. With the Privy Council's advice she would formally approve and sign acts of Parliament, orders of council, international agreements and constitutional queries, proclamations and financial documents for the transfer of government funds. This is likely to be followed by the hosting of a lunch, which can either be a formal lunch with a guest such as President George Bush when he visited London in 1997, or informal lunches where the Queen invites people from a range of occupations.

In addition to publicised events she also attends a weekly meeting with the Prime Minister. While Parliament is convening, at 7.30 in the evening, a report of the day's parliamentary proceedings arrives at Buckingham Palace, which is read by the Queen the same evening. And all this does not take into account official state ceremonies such as the Opening of Parliament, investitures or visits from foreign royals.

Republicanism

There have always been two main arguments for introducing a republican style of government to the UK but neither holds up to detailed scrutiny. The first is the question of suitability. The argument is that birthright is no guarantee of character. The problem is that an elected President is no guarantee of character either, particularly as most candidates are likely to be politicians, while a hereditary monarch remains neutral to party politics.

The second argument used by republicans is the cost of monarchy. The Queen receives £7.9 million annually towards the running costs of her office and staff, upon which she now pays income tax. This is only slightly more than the combined salaries of Mr Blair's special advisors. It would almost certainly cost more to set up a presidential office, with an additional cost of £45 million every time Britain elected a new President. As a comparison, the British government managed to spend £860[7] million on the millennium dome. It may seem obsequious to compare Britain's monarch to a building but it could be legitimately asked which of the two institutions has given more value to Britain?

Elizabeth II took an oath to protect and serve her people for life without the possibility of retirement. Abolishing the monarch would simply make the executive more powerful. Britain's monarchy has lasted 1600 years and replacing it with an elected President is unlikely to bring stability. Constitutional change is a natural process, but the introduction of direct democracy ought not to threaten the monarchy for two reasons. The first is that for many British people Elizabeth II epitomises hard work and integrity, but more importantly, Queen Elizabeth remains a constitutional check against the excesses of government.

SECTION FOUR

King Snear

ACT I SCENE I

A FIELD SOME MILES FROM BRUSSELIOS

TWIT

That what I now knowest, is a frozen morn,
Thou hadst a pain on the ear, a weeping nose to guide,
I have a presence to slow, like a whipped horse follow'n.
His velvet tail through town, dale, field and shit,
A platform for his chattels and a silent drum to beat,
May this inclemency, crack the knob off thi' master's stick.

SNEAR

Twit, nay stay not to witter,
We are treading down the night,
Darkness and danger on the wing,
Stalks our movement, so give rest to thee tongue,
Or may challenge this thick ash, to your thicker skull.
[aside] A clerk should know, a proper place,
Not to trifle with this cup, for stars say I am prone,
To land on my back, tasting destinie's sweet draught.

TWIT

> Sorry my virtuous Lord, cold hath make my mind slow,
> Oh I would rather stand with thee on a field,
> Than wit a thousand fine Englishmen, with taut bows,
> Good master indeed, you are an eloquence of a speaker,
> If I had an edi ... cation in my head, I might aspire,
> Indeed it would like, as, 'avin jam on my bread,'

SNEAR

> A heart of lard, nay soul of lard, brain of lard,
> But it may show compliant promise,
> For a lamb may lie on our tray of treatise,
> For I carry in my head a parchment,
> With no consent, I know how to be bettered,
> My eyes, with no greater game of chance,
> I will practise to sell on and be made good.

TWIT

> Up ahead Sir a lace of stone, atop a mound,
> Wit holes next my feet, let us hope this is it,
> Or my employment, be gainful no more,
> Like a pile on my rear side, too much to bare.

SNEAR

> Look up, it draws us towards our journey's end,
> Good day, we bring tidings,
> From our Queen greetings,
> From her minions cheap trinkets,
> And myself ignoble expectations.

THE CASTLE OF BRUSSELIOS IS NOW IN VIEW

GUARD

> Look my league, a caravan of stately colours,
> Atop a horse a noble, wif fine feathers atop a hat,
> Nah, a servant behind, wif feathers in his ears,
> For I hear him complain, at two hundred span,
> Load the braziers with red beef to burn black,
> For they are from the English breed of dog,
> Open the gates to piss on them below!

ACT II SCENE I

THE BANQUETING HALL

TWIT

> My eyes a fixed amongst splendour,
> Tis silver plate and more food than people,
> My pocket itches but hanging is a scratch too dear,
> While they make work of talking no sense,
> I shall eat my fill, once my master is distracted.

SNEAR

> Your holiness and virtue walk in one person,
> Tis the earth that warm, and sparkle under flat feet,
> Thine fame has travelled to our shores,
> 'My people sing your praises from their crofts,
> Two hundred miles, a small tally now forgotton!
> For these tired eyes, have been refreshed,
> On seeing wisdom, in such abundance.

BURO

You are clear with your voice, and compliments,
Accustomed to 1 of none, doth the moon need heat?
Or the spider pity, when silking the fly?
And a man to come, with no hidden price?
For you tally in Brusselios, what game play thea?
1 have no room left for verse, 1 can call many,
Bidding to the sweet rhythm of my sword.

SNEAR

1 have a good notion, a mere treaty,
That we eat riches, beyond our dreamin,
Among a few, 1 have spiked a quiet vow,
Stealth, promise and pike will see it through,
To smear the reward, far from others,

TWIT

Did 1 hear my master hath a good motion?
Full of stones and worms more like,
For this food look sweet, then taste of foul onion,
Oh for Welsh ale and Scotch beef on my lips,
1 would walk home, on these birthday knees

BURO

Snear doth touch my ego, ne'er satisfied,
For God's speed and my embroidered coat,
Hath new when rags we all dealt,
Be a jester, nay a twisted airy tongue?
Or a wooden casket, full of air?
Impute your mind, for my confidence alone.

SNEAR

A lump of rock, no more than... chalk,
With gentlemen and mock tournaments in mind,
Of gentle folk with straw between their ears,
Easy wooed and merry hung this year,
For the taking, with a single quill against iron,
An erection of plinth, with thou frame in mind,
And mine too when the day hath gone.

TWIT

Thith wine be better, wunf a bottle gone,
For my lord an erection like a plinth he plan,
Saying to honour, my good friends at home?

BURO

Holy knelled twas bells, shall be swung,
For we lov'd this life, so much to waste,
A deal we done, so your word I will wait,
To wreak havoc upon our allies,
Bid safe crossing, on that short sea.

SNEAR

I now bid thee farewell, my good Snear.

INTERLUDE

ACT III Scene I

THE PALACE OF LONDON

MAJESTY

What doth bring noble Lord Snear, 'potato or baccy'!

SNEAR

More than just nosh, your grace,
Our foes, have lain down ink to draw peace,
A small price paid but not so hard to bare,
Just words, under your reign of course,
So this gain may, take a final form,
[aside] Nay I say one thing to them, another you!

MAJESTY

But what price thee, Buro haggles well I know,
Yet you speak well, I suppose of this,
Be a trusted fellow, in this court and land,
For all good men, will know their friend,
Sleep with gentle eyes, for no guard required,
As our ships moor and sailors sing,
Sing the praise of Snear, from gate to knell.

SNEAR

Twas a small price, from such a rich throne,
Chipped away slowly, will surely be gone,
To rattle with worms and bones in a crypt,
Or dead flower heads, on dunghill deep!

MAJESTY

And where of servant Twit?
A stout fellow in size, not sense or guile,
Like a mule to grumble and stomach too!
Did he not follow, into your same dawn?
Or board the planks for Dover's loin?

SNEAR

He was but common, with no sense of shame,
Upset our foreign fellows, for earthly gain,
Found pockets of gold, took from our friends,
No matter he was hung, high on a tree.
[aside] Twas really an ear, that could hear my secret gain,
So planted with stealth, drunk there was no pain.

❧

FINAL SCENE

TWIT'S GHOST

Yeah no matter, my Lord Snear,
Though we fear, we take your hand,
And though was clammy, be held tight,
To rejoice and gait into the night,
Our poor future, now ith bright,
Long may our land, enjoy free reign,
Three cheers for Lord Snear's gain!

CURTAIN

Chapter Eight

✔

The European Union

The European Union now has enormous powers and influence over the people of Europe, yet many people are unaware of the background to its rapid expansion. The concept of a united Europe has been around since Roman times but it wasn't until the sixteenth century that serious thought was given to the idea of political unification. What Europe had experienced were various attempts to integrate Europe using military power by groups, such as the Bourbons, the Hapsburgs and later Napoleon. Postwar European unification has been more successful largely because it is perceived as benign.

Between the two world wars a French statesmen called Aristide Briand had proposed the ill-timed concept of a European Federal Union, but the Second World War would halt this political vision. Post 1945 with two thirds of the population of Europe refugees, and many people with no means of earning a living, politicians such as Paul-Henri Spaak and Jean Monnet began to look again at ways of securing Europe's future. These dreams were again curbed by the growing Soviet ambitions towards Eastern Europe.

With Britain's economy close to bankruptcy, America saw the rebuilding of Europe's economic and defence infrastructure as a priority. Between 1948 and 1951, the United States contributed $13.2 billion to European reconstruction projects, which also acted as a counterbalance against Soviet influence in Europe.[1] Winston Churchill had spoken with the American President - Harry S. Truman of the need to 'recreate th̶e̶ ̶European family,' and 'provide it with a structure ̶̶̶̶̶̶̶̶̶̶̶̶̶̶̶ ̶̶peace, safety and in freedom.' Althou̶g̶h̶ ̶h̶i̶s̶ ̶w̶o̶r̶d̶s̶ ̶h̶a̶v̶e̶ often ̶been misinterpreted, Churchill was hoping that britain might become a diplomatic bridge between Europe and the United States, rather than part of a European state. As he later said:

> 'We have our own dream and our own task, we are with Europe but not of it. We are linked but not compromised.'[2]

By 1949, despite serious misgivings by the British government, a Council of Europe was set up under the chairmanship of Paul-Henri Spaak. What was intended as a sharing of ideas, soon became nothing more than a talking shop. Monnet later summed up the conference by saying, 'it was a gathering of people expressing general views and going home. This suited many European countries as it was felt that while the Germans and French were talking, it greatly reduced the risk of further military conflict.

Jean Monnet, whose career had started in business rather than politics, approached the French Prime Minister Bidault with a proposal to drive forward European integration under the guise of commerce. As he stated, 'We are starting a process of continuous reform…which can shape tomorrow's world more lastingly than the principles of revolution so widespread outside the West.'[3] Monnet was fully aware that his proposals were controversial, so by emphasising the commercial aspects of the plan it was made more palatable to the European electorate, while disguising the true implications.

Nearly 40 per cent of Europe's coal reserves were situated in the Ruhr Valley and the surrounding area but the German surrender treaty had placed these under international administration. Monnet suggested that French and German coal and steel industries might be run under the umbrella of a new European Coal and Steel Community based in Luxembourg. The Germans were desperate for diplomatic recognition, while the French saw an opportunity to remove the control of vital resources away from Germany. Once Germany had lost control of its coal and steel industries it would be almost impossible to wage war on France.

The European coal and steel community

In 1967 the European Coal and Steel Community (ECSC) was born, removing all economic tariffs between participating members and reducing competition within the two industries. With hindsight this move can be viewed as a method of protectionism against those suppliers who remained outside the group. Not surprisingly, neither Britain nor the United States participated. Britain had large natural reserves of coal and did not envisage giving up control of steel production. As Her Majesty's government pointed out,

> 'The future treaty which you are discussing, has no chance of being agreed; if it were agreed, it would have no chance of being ratified; if it were ratified, it would have no chance of being applied. And if it were applied, it would be totally unacceptable to Britain.'[4]

America, too, was sensitive about the implications of the ECSC on its own coal and steel export - but Monnet had greater ambitions for Europe. Soon after the ECSC was initiated, he began campaigning for a European Defence Community, an Executive Commissariat, a Council of Ministers, an Assembly and a European High Court, which he felt should come under the heading of a European Political Community. Ironically, these plans faltered when they came up against the implacable force of the French Nationalists, led by Général Charles de Gaulle, and the Communists in the French National Assembly. Both groups were concerned about the loss of French identity and the fear that Germany would gain too much influence over European policy. Monnet, disappointed that his plans had faltered, moved out of mainstream politics to set up an independent campaign for European political integration. Described by one diplomat as a 'mixture of gangster and conspirator',[5] Monnet would come to play an increasingly influential role in the future of Europe.

By 1955, in a country house just outside Brussels, a proposal was launched under the chairmanship of Paul-Henri Spaak to create what was to be known as the European Market and an organisation to oversee a European atomic energy programme. Both the Germans and the French had agendas that were important to their future development. Germany was still an outcast in international politics, while France desperately wanted nuclear technology as it lagged further and further behind the United States, Russia and Britain.

By March 1957 Spaak's minutes and summary of the meeting were reworded in a legal style, and the European Economic Community (EEC) and the European Atomic Energy Community (EURATOM) were formerly proposed. Following an elaborate ceremony in Rome and a considerable amount of behind-the-scenes political dealing, the Treaty of Rome came into effect on the 1 January 1958.

Britain's Parliament

Britain's Prime Minister Harold Macmillan was hoping to convince France and Germany of an alternative free-trade agreement, which had been entitled the 'G Plan'. French and German politicians showed little interest as they felt that they had a scheme that would eventually rival the political structure of the United States. In 1960 the British government had a cabinet reshuffle, with three pro-European ministers moving into positions of influence. Lord Home, Edward Heath and Duncan Sandys. They were all to play a key role in Britain's affairs with Europe over the coming years.

In 1961 Britain made a formal application to join what was being described as the 'Common Market' of Europe. The British public were told that this was going to be a European trading arrangement. French President Charles de Gaulle's priority was to establish the European Economic Community as an independent power against American economic interests. The Germans and Italians soon made it obvious that they were uncomfortable with the way that de Gaulle was dominating the agenda. The Benelux countries (Belgium, the Netherlands and Luxembourg) were unhappy to proceed without the agreement of Britain.

In Britain, public opinion changed from being mildly sympathetic to outright hostile, when it became clear that the Northern European Countries would be heavily subsidising the Southern European Countries for many years to come. But Edward Heath was resolute about Britain's future in Europe, as he said, 'when public opinion is uncertain about something, as it was about Europe at that time, what is required is not an abdication of leadership but more leadership.'[6] Meanwhile behind the scenes, British diplomats negotiated a financially disastrous membership package.

Although the argument for free trade was used to convince the European public of the case for Europe, another agenda soon came to light. As Edward Heath was later to admit, 'We have all recognised that the Treaties of Rome and Paris had a political as well as an economic objective.'[7] and later he said 'the primary reason why Britain entered into these negotiations was political, political in its widest sense.'[8] The British public had been duped into believing, that the Common Market was a trading agreement. In reality many of the important political figures involved were aware that the aim was to create an integrated political state.

Then in 1963, Britain's attempts to join the Common Market received a slap in the face. On 14 January at the Elysée Palace, President de Gaulle announced to an incredulous audience that he would be blocking Britain's entry to the Common Market. He followed this announcement with sweeping criticisms of Britain's nuclear programme. Despite this anti-nuclear display, de Gaulle was secretly developing a nuclear programme using technology that had been covertly acquired. Representatives from the other European countries - who had not been consulted by De Gaulle - were furious. Once it became clear that this was a formal veto by de Gaulle the proceedings were wound up.

The 1970s

Edward Heath, the leader of the Conservative Party, became Prime Minister in 1970. In his maiden speech to Parliament, Edward Heath had made Europe central to his vision for a New Britain. He had himself served during the Second World war and felt that Europe's defence and security lay in closer cooperation within Europe. He also felt Europe was the best way to introduce modern industrial practices into Britain, as it had increasingly fallen behind its European competitors. Germany, whose industrial base had been completely destroyed, had the advantage of rebuilding its industry with the most modern equipment available, while at the same time introducing more efficient working practises.

At a meeting with President Pompidou in May 1971, Edward Heath made it clear that Britain wanted to be a committed member of the European Community. However, in Britain he faced increasingly fierce opposition from the Trade Unions, the public and his own Conservative Party. The financial cost of membership for Britain turned out to be much higher than originally anticipated because of the way that contributions were calculated and, although Heath's strategy was that this could be changed later, it was to haunt the British economy for many years to come.

In 1979 Britain was one of the least prosperous members of the community. The Gross Domestic Product per head of the population meant that Britain ranked seventh in the community, yet it was going to become the largest net contributor. A Common Fisheries Policy was also smuggled through which traded off the British fishing industry for political agreement with the other European partners. By 1974 Britain's economy had been brought to its knees by striking coal miners, and the public voted Edward Heath's Conservative Party out of government, bringing in Harold Wilson's Labour government.

The Labour Party

From the opposition benches Harold Wilson had led an increasingly anti-European Labour Party, with the majority of Labour's trade union and constituency support against membership of Europe. Wilson was ambivalent but used the idea of a national referendum to seek a consensus between his warring backbenchers. By permitting his home secretary to campaign for a 'yes' vote on Europe, he was able to placate the pro-Europeans within his party. In the face of public disquiet, he emphasised the financial benefits of the Common Market by spending huge amounts of taxpayers' money campaigning for a 'yes' vote. At the same time he made it clear that he 'would not be bound by the result,' which made a mockery of the whole exercise.[9]

From Wilson's point of view the campaign was a success: the

public agreed to membership of the Common Market and the 'yes' vote reduced dissent within Wilson's Labour government. The problem was the British public had voted for a free trade agreement, but European membership had wider implications. By the 1970s it became clear that the Common Market, which had subtly been renamed the European Economic Community (EEC), was not performing as well as it had hoped against its main rivals America and Japan. At the same time, Britain was struggling to rebuild its ageing industries, while contributing a disproportionate amount of money.

Worst of all for Britain, of the EEC's huge budget, 45 per cent was spent on agricultural subsidies which Britain received little of because of its relatively efficient farming system. The public became increasingly cynical, as they were forced to pay higher prices for commodities such as butter and milk, while millions of tons of food were dumped in holes or left to rot on farms. By 1979 the EEC needed unanimous authorisation among its members to raise more money but Britain had a new Prime Minister, Margaret Thatcher had no intention of handing over more cash! She harangued her fellow Europeans with the demand for 'our money back', and was eventually rewarded when some financial redress was made to Britain.

Towards a single currency

In 1985 Jacques Delors arrived on the European political scene. Seen by some as a colourful technocrat, he was a highly skilled and wily negotiator. Like Monnet, Delours saw the European Market as the first step towards a European Federal State that would in time subsume all of its members into a wider European government. These ideas would mature into the Single European Act of 1987, which extended the areas covered by majority voting. Mrs

Thatcher was unusually slow on the uptake, over the implications of these proposals, having been told by her own ministers that majority voting was needed to curb the misuse of power by some smaller European members. The Single European Act came into being on the 1 July 1987.

At the same time, plans had begun for a European Central Bank and a European currency. At a summit in Strasbourg on 8 December 1987, the French and Germans had reached an implicit deal that European Monetary Union should be introduced by the end of 1990. Chancellor Helmut Kohl of Germany faced considerable opposition from the German public and the Bundesbank, which feared the loss of the extremely reliable Deutschmark and of Germany's influence. The German people and the Bundesbank were promised, that any countries that failed to meet the strict criteria of European Monetary Union would be severely penalised.

This later proved to be wishful thinking, after various currencies failed to meet the criteria were quietly excused. This was to the dismay of those countries that had endured economic hardship to keep their currencies within the European Union's 'strict' criteria. Using European Monetary Union as a pretext, negotiations were then started on subjects as wide ranging as education, culture, health and the environment. These were described in official European documents as 'new competencies,' making them appear more palatable to the voters of Europe. As we know, the first attempt at European Monetary Union - with its financial vehicle the Exchange Rate Mechanism - was to be a spectacular and costly disaster.

As Bernard Connolly explained, Exchange Rate Mechanism was:

'a mechanism for subordinating the economic welfare, democratic rights and national freedoms of citizens of the European countries to the will of political bureaucratic elites, whose power-lust, cynicism and delusions underlie the actions of the vast majority of those who strive to create a European super state.'[10]

This was not the criticism of an outsider, as Mr Connolly was the Head of the European Commission's group responsible for the analysis of the European Monetary System. That was until he published a book explaining what was happening with European Monetary policy and he was duly sacked!

Maastricht

The pretty, but unassuming, Dutch town of Maastricht was to give its name to a treaty that became known as 'Maastricht's hidden treaty,' as so many of its proposals were disguised within its baffling terminology. The Maastricht Treaty, officially 'the Treaty of the European Union', came into being in 1992, and it sets out the most ambitious plan for political integration that the continent of Europe has ever seen. Within its remit it encompasses planned economic and monetary union, justice and home affairs policies, common foreign and security policies and the integration of social and employment legislation. It also introduced, for the first time, a new word - 'subsidiarity.' The EU's definition of subsidiarity is the:

'principle whereby the Union does not take action, except in the areas which fall within its exclusive competence, unless it is more effective than action taken at national, regional or local level.'

A BBC journalist who reviewed the treaty described it as a 'supreme piece of political mumbo jumbo, as it meant whatever you wanted it to mean and it was devilishly hard to define in legal terms'. Behind the bureaucratically legal language, the Maastricht treaty gave the EU, incredibly wide ranging powers, over national governments and the electorate of Europe.

In Britain the Prime Minister John Major made a show of gaining an opt-out on some of the EU's social clauses, while signing away much of Westminster's sovereign right to make legislation. What was also added was another change of name, from the European Economic Community to the European Union (EU). The point at which the people of Europe were consulted over whether they wanted to become 'citizens of Europe' remains unclear.

Desperate times

Amid all this political testosterone there was black cloud moving in on the horizon. On 16 September 1992, Italy was knocked out of the Exchange Rate Mechanism and Spain was forced to rapidly devalue its currency. John Major's Chancellor, Norman Lamont, had viewed membership of the Exchange Rate Mechanism as integral to his anti-inflationary policies. However he was not to reckon on the lack of cooperation he would receive, as the British pound was not allowed to revalue against the Deutschmark. The real victims of the chaos were the millions of homeowners across Europe who lost their homes and the multitude of businesses that went bankrupt.

The fall of the British Sterling from the Exchange Rate Mechanism cost billions of pounds, as the government attempted to support sterling by buying it far above its real value on the international markets. Britain alone lost an estimated £30 billion. Money that could have been used to pay for schools, hospitals or simply to reduce the UK's tax burden. Many of the protagonists of what might be considered, one of the worst examples of financial mismanagement in British history were later punished by being exiled to the House of Lords.

By 2001 the Euro currency was launched across much of Europe, despite a wave of popular opposition, including the rejection of the currency by the people of Denmark, who were fearful of losing their parliamentary sovereignty. On the continent of Europe, within two years prices had increased by a staggering 25 per cent in real terms and the European Central Bank, responsible for controlling inflation, was forced to issue an economic warning that the situation had 'worsened significantly.'[11] Britain's Prime Minister Tony Blair has since told the EU that subject to a successful launch of the Euro and a favourable referendum, Britain would be joining the Euro at some point in the next Parliament. Months have turned into years, and still a date for the promised referendum has failed to materialise.

Conclusion

Some of the original reasons for moving towards European integration were based on a genuine desire to build a more secure Europe. The problem is that in the 1940s it would have been impossible for anyone to foresee the geo-political structure of the world sixty years on. Threats to European security no longer come from the Soviet bloc but from global terrorism, catastrophic environmental change and the misuse of power by unaccountable bodies. The expansion of Europe has not been driven by popular support but by the ambitions of an unpopular elite, whose schemes have been presented to the electorate as non-negotiable.

Although the dream of European integration was sparked by the experience of war, history has repeatedly shown us that conflict is more likely when power is concentrated in the hands of a few. Having agreed to what is now an unaccountable bureaucracy above the sovereignty of nation states, the people of Europe have left themselves vulnerable. European nations would have a safer check on tyranny by retaining their own sovereignty, rather than relying on a European government with little credibility and even less public support. The proposed plan for a Federal Europe can not be described as democratic and could lead to the destabilisation of Europe, as elected politicians increasingly ignore the wishes of the electorate.

Surely it is only reasonable that the electorate of Europe should be consulted over their wishes and acted upon? Of course the European project moves on as the EU welcomes ten new member countries. It begs two important questions. First, where will the geographical ambitions of the European Union end? And second, who is going to subsidise its expansion? To the first question, no one seems to have an answer. To the second, it is likely that again it will be the Western European States who will carry the burden.

Chapter Nine

✔

What Difference Does It Make?

Many decisions that are made by the EU are done with little or no consultation with the people of Europe. Indeed there seems to be a growing disquiet over the loss of many aspects of the diverse culture that individual European states have always provided. Of course some countries have benefited financially from becoming members of the European Union but whether a highly bureaucratic European government has been of overall benefit is doubtful. Much of the European budget is spent on administration and protectionism in the form of subsidies that have kept European prices artificially high.

Since joining in 1972, the UK is estimated to have paid a staggering £600 billion in real terms, yet like many European countries it has only received back a fraction of this through the EU's complex and bureaucratic system of fund reallocation. Many of the decisions taken on the nation's behalf certainly appear detrimental to it. Let us look at some of these points in more detail:

It doesn't make any difference being in the EU.
As an example, the average British family now contributes around £2,600 to the EU every year in direct subsidies and indirect taxation such as VAT. The question is, given the choice, would the public choose to spend their money in this way. An opinion poll on

10th January 1997, found that only 34 per cent of Britons regard membership of the EU as a good thing.[1]

The EU costs less than people realise.

Britain only receives a fraction of the money that it puts into the EU. Of the money that is returned it is under EU direction and is poorly administered. One audit which looked at the EU's 'Urban Initiative' found that 'projects supported under this initiative could equally well have been carried out under existing Community measures,' avoiding 'the creation of new procedures and management structures.'

The irony is that the UK is already paying for a similar project of its own, as the report says, '[in] Britain the Single Regeneration Budget programme supports similar projects to those under the 'URBAN' initiative. Lack of coordination between such projects had in some cases led to a proliferation of interventions and an increase in management costs.'[2]

Talk of fraud in the EU is just propaganda.

There have been many well-documented cases of fraud, costing billions of Euros. One report showed that 'in relation to agriculture, common types of fraud involved the manipulation of quota systems or set-aside programmes... in relation to structural measures, cases of fraud often involved the use of false invoices and false declarations by project beneficiaries.'[3]

The EU government is representative.

In the UK only 25 per cent of those eligible to vote did so in the European Elections of 1999 and this apathy is common all across Europe. Yet those who did not vote were not taken into account, as they had no other way of voicing their concerns. Across Europe, political parties advocating independence from the EU have received substantial popular support.

The EU is democratic!

European MPs who are democratically elected have little influence over the important decisions that are taken. As Paul van Buitenen writes:

> 'As citizens of Europe we elect a European Parliament every five years. The democratically elected body only has a limited power of decision. In fact, the real power still lies with the national governments. The important decisions are taken by the Council Of Ministers. However, national parliaments have no democratic control over the Council's decisions.'[4]

The EU is not moving towards a federal super state.

As Jean Monnet said as long ago as 1958, 'the everyday realities will make it possible to form the political union, which is the goal of our Community and to establish the United States of Europe.'[5]

The UK relies on Europe for trade.

The UK imports more goods from Europe than it exports to Europe. In fact Britain exports more goods to countries outside the EU. Norway and Switzerland have remained independent of the EU politically and have retained trading agreements with Europe, while becoming two of the most affluent nations in the world, per head of the population.[6]

The EU produces good legislation.

Not all of the EU is defective, but it seems odd that countries that have been able to run their own affairs for thousands of years should need someone else to make its laws? As an example, regulation within Britain's industries and services already accounts for 9 per cent of industrial costs. The UK's Institute of Directors esti-mates that of this 60 per cent is due to EU regulations.[7]

Europeans need the EU to remain competitive.

The EU has embarked on the road of trade protectionism but world trading patterns are changing. Soon Europe will be faced with the might of nations such as China and India becoming indus-trial superpowers. Artificially protecting European industries will in the long term fail, as companies will trade with those who can offer the best services at the best prices.

In the future what will be important is focusing on a high-value, knowledge-driven economy. Taxpayers across Europe are already paying the price with artificially higher prices. This is evident to anyone who travels to Asia or the United States, where prices are much lower for the same commodities.

The UK doesn't want to be left out of the EU's 'exciting' political expansion.

Cyprus, Estonia, Hungary, Latvia, Lithuania, Malta, Poland, the Slovak Republic, the Czech Republic, and Slovenia have now all completed negotiations to become full members of Europe. Romania and Bulgaria are presently negotiating membership and negotiations have begun with Turkey. The problem is that the people of the nation states of Europe have not been consulted and there is little real enthusiasm for these changes.

The EU is needed for national security.

Most Western European countries are already members of NATO, which states quite clearly that if one NATO member is attacked the others are committed to go to its defence. NATO has protected Europe for over fifty years, and talk of an EU army is only serving to undermine NATO's allies. The United States spends more money on the defence of Europe than all of the EU countries put together![8]

The war in Yugoslavia gave us some idea of what would happen if Europe were to be left in charge of its own defence arrangements. European politicians spent four years discussing what it might do until the United States lost patience and intervened on Europe's behalf.[9] Even then, of the EU countries only Britain managed to send the requested 2 per cent of armed forces. As one MP pointed out, if an EU army were to become a reality in the future, Britain could be faced with the nightmare scenario of the EU's central executive declaring war on the rebel area of Norfolk.

Talk of an EU army is ridiculous.
The Maastricht Treaty specifically states that 'security policy shall include all questions related to the security of the Union, including the eventual framing of a common defence policy, which might in time lead to a common defence, thereby reinforcing the European identity and its independence.' Although hidden in the text, the intention is clear.

A European police force would never be created.
'Work is underway to create "Eurojust", a judicial co-operation unit involving magistrates, prosecutors and police officers across the European Community, and a provisional unit (Pro-Eurojust) started work in March 2001. "Eurojust" is intended to facilitate the proper coordination of national prosecuting authorities and support criminal investigations in cases of serious organised crime across national borders.'[10]

Talk of an EU criminal court is just that - all talk.
'In December 2001, the Commission issued a consultative Green

Paper on the establishment of an European Public Prosecutor to protect the Community's financial interests under criminal law. The European Public Prosecutor would be an independent judicial authority empowered to conduct investigations and prosecutions anywhere in Europe into offences against the Community's financial interests.'[11]

Talk of setting up EU embassies is ridiculous.
The European, Commission which represents the EU in Britain, has set up a page on its website which details 'EU Embassies and tourist offices.' Although they are based within nation state embassies, the implication is clearly that they are acting as embassies for the European Union.[12] Many embassies across Europe are now displaying the EU flag alongside their own national flags.

Talk of the EU raising taxes is just too far-fetched.
The European Union already effectively controls VAT and customs and excise rates and it adds tariffs on to goods and services entering the EU, such as sugar. One report noted that:

> 'VAT and GNP contributions to the European Community were based on macro economic statistics, calculated at Member State level... which represented over 80 per cent of Community revenue in 2000.'[13]

It is not as though Europeans are expected to be citizens of the EU.
According to the Maastricht Treaty of 1992 they already are! The European Union changed the definition of itself from a 'community' to a 'union.' In 2004 the Labour government undertook plans to introduce an EU constitution into UK law, even before the

UK has its own written constitution! The difficulty is that unlike the United States of America, the United States of Europe would be artificial and motivated by politicians who are out of step with public opinion.

The EU is needed for political stability.
We have already seen the rise of extreme right-wing groups in Southern France, Germany and Austria. We could potentially face the scenario of a civil struggle across Europe because politicians are not prepared to listen to the public's concerns.

Countries have only gained from being in the EU.
It is difficult to see what most European countries have gained that they would not have gained from a simple trade agreement, such as Norway or Switzerland already has with the EU.

The EU doesn't employ as many bureaucrats as is often portrayed.
That is because so many are appointed as special advisors and outside consultants. Therefore, they do not have to appear on the EU's employee statistics.

We don't want to miss the boat!
This might have been said of the last person who boarded the Titanic! There is one sensible way to improve the well being of European nation states, and that is with a reduction in government bureaucracy, better working practices and by innovating and producing goods and services that other countries want to buy. Being a member of a 'special' club such as the EU will never be a short cut to affluence.

This all sounds Europhobic!
There are as many Germans, Danish, French, Belgians, Italians,

Dutch and so on, who are also concerned about what's happening in Europe. Our major criticism of the EU is its unaccountability. It is under no legal obligation to act in accordance with the wishes of the European public.

The EU government can be trusted to look after different nations' interests.

In 1988 in the Factorame case the British government was fined £100 million for trying to protect its own fishing grounds from over fishing by foreign trawlers.[14] For every job lost by a British fisherman, five jobs were lost onshore and it is estimated that the UK has now lost a total of 150,000 jobs due to EU fishing policies.

Three years after the European beef ban was lifted France was still refusing to import British beef, yet the EU took no effective action. At the same time it was widely accepted that BSE (mad cow disease) existed in both French and Irish beef herds! The total cost to the British taxpayer was around £3.5 billion, yet Britain received no compensation from the EU.[15]

Then most controversially, in 2001, the European Court of Human Rights awarded compensation to the families of IRA activists who were shot dead by an SAS ambush as they attempted to bomb Loughgall police station in County Armagh in 1987. British taxpayers were then faced with a bill for £400,000 in compensation and costs. The European Court of Human Rights' judgement was described by the Northern Ireland Executive as 'astonishing and perverse'.[16]

Not having the Euro would destroy the City of London's financial centre.

London is an international market. It is successful because it has a strict professional code and it is effective in regulating itself. In the

1970s the US imposed a tax, similar to that being envisaged by the EU on European money markets. The consequence was that US funds were quickly transferred to London. If more restrictions were placed on the City of London much of this trade would simply move to Asia. Ironically, the City of London has made money out of the Euro, even though the pound is Britain's official currency. 'The Bank of England reported that London's share of Euro denominated bond markets grew from 48 per cent to 58 per cent between the first and third quarters of 1999 alone.'[17]

Business needs the Euro to increase competition.

The estimated cost of introducing the Euro to Britain would be in the region of £9 billion.[18] A report by Goldman Sachs stated that 'the degree of fiscal tightening foreseen by Goldman equates to raising taxes by about £10 billion - roughly 3p on income tax.'[19] In Europe the Euro has caused substantial price increases in real terms. We can compare the Euro to the last decimalisation that took place where inflation soared and prices increased by around 10 per cent over a period of one year.

Fiona Tankard, a writer living in Italy, who had seen at first hand the effect of that the Euro's introduction has said, 'locals and visitors alike complain of noticeable rises in their weekly shopping and in restaurants and hotels of up to 10 per cent.'[20] This though is not what the public across Europe has been told by the EU. As Adair Turner, Director General of the CBI, said, 'I think "the European public" have been given false assurances that EMU itself will directly create jobs and cure unemployment - an assertion without intellectual justification.'[21]

All of Europe has the Euro.

In Denmark on 28 September 2000 the Danish public - a little more savvy to what was happening - rejected the Euro with the view that their long-standing tradition of freedom and democracy should remain with their own Parliament[22] Denmark was the first country to offer its people a referendum on the subject; many others simply passed the measure without consultation. The courageous Danes struck a chord across Europe, as other countries started to demand a referendum on the Euro. In the UK, even though the public had been promised a referendum, the government soon buried the idea when it realised that it would more than likely lose a referendum.

The Euro is helpful when travelling abroad.
Most people have to wait for two hours at the airport prior to travelling, more than enough time to change currencies. People who travel frequently are more likely to use credit cards. Besides, the no-thrills airline Ryan Air has recently discovered that the EU is planning to abolish low-cost flights under the guise of anti-competition laws![23] Michael O'Leary, Ryan Air's chief executive, described the EU's economic interference as 'evil'. At the same time, the EU subsidises a variety of chosen industries against outside competition using European tax money.

Some of the press reports about Europe are just make believe.
Many stories are based on genuine legislation and real EU directives. After some research we managed to track down the fabled straight cucumber directive. It is in fact Directive number 1677/88 of 15 June 1988, which lays down quality standards for cucumbers. It says within its eighteen pages (in eight languages) that cucumbers shall 'be well shaped and practically straight (maximum height of the arc 10mm per 10cm of length of the cucumber), have a typical colouring of the variety, be free of defects,

including all deformations and particularly those caused by seed formation.'[24] Did European taxpayers' money really need to be spent stating the obvious?

Many global corporations support the Euro.
Of course there are some companies claiming that the introduction of the Euro to the UK is essential. Companies such as Nissan UK - which kept quiet after it was pointed out that they were 37 per cent owned by the French company Renault![25]

There is no alternative to the EU
The European public does have an alternative but they have never been offered it. European nations could become fully independent and negotiate a common trading arrangement. Norway and Switzerland are not part of the EU and they both enjoy successful economies. If change does not occur many areas within Europe are likely to become federal backwaters, valued for their cheap labour and as a useful place for dumping the welfare problems of Europe.

Chapter Ten

✔

The EU and the Missing Millions

At the beginning of 1998 an assistant auditor working for the European Commission published a book that showed a level of fraud, corruption and incompetence within the EU that would shock even the European Community's most ardent supporters. Paul van Buitenen's book, Blowing the Whistle, became an international bestseller, yet the British government had little to say about it. Certainly many Europeans remained unaware of his findings. What Paul van Buitenen found was that millions of pounds of taxpayers' money was being illegally diverted into front companies and unqualified consultants with the knowledge of some of the most senior staff at the EU.

When managers realised what van Buitenen had discovered, he was moved to other departments where it was more difficult for him to have access to records. He faced personal threats, intimidation and even attempts to discredit his mental health. As he later acknowledged, what he found was probably only the tip of the iceberg yet without people like him who have had the courage to speak out, Europeans would still not be aware of what is happening. The UK's National Audit Office produced two damning reports of the EU's accounting practices and, although carefully worded, it found a plethora of inadequacies in the EU's accounting procedures.

In its summary it said:

'objectives were often poorly defined and evaluation by the
Commission of the achievement of objectives was inadequate…
there remain significant problems which prevent better management, reduction of administrative cost.'[1]

Eventually the media took up the story and the appalling details
were to lead to the whole of the EU Commission resigning.

Outside contractors

The initial criticism revolved around the way that the EU uses outside contracting companies to carry out its policies. To give the
impression that it does not employ too many staff, it has devised a
rather ingenious system whereby full-time Commission staff are
grouped under Directorates-General. These Directorates-General
have various roles but are backed up by innumerable outside consultants and temporary staff (being independent they do not have
to appear on records as full-time staff.) The Directorates-General
essentially tender out EU programmes to independent organisations that are known as Technical Assistance Offices (TAOs).

These TAOs then carry out EU projects for a prearranged contract fee that they have agreed with the Directorates-General.
Once the policy guidelines of the programme have been set in place
the Directorates-General have little involvement again with the
TAOs. The TAOs are supposed to tender for quotes to carry out
these programmes so that the best value option can be chosen.
These TAOs should be run independently but some contractors
were actually allowed to write their tenders within the departments.[2]

Other contractors were tipped off in advance that a particular
programme was to be set up or EU technical assistants were on

hand to advise on how to write a suitable tender. Even though this amounts to fraud, criminal proceedings were not implemented for fear that it might be leaked to the press. On occasions when cases of fraud were uncovered, staff were often moved to avoid bad publicity.

British auditors found a series of anomalies when looking at the EU's yearly accounts. Some of the points were:

- the EU court could not give assurances on reliability![3]

- misstatements of values of certain fixed assets and 'inadequately defined policies on the calculation and write-off of bad debts.'[4]

- the Commission had not been able to produce complete and reliable information between advance and final payments.[5]

- there was a lack of clarity to the extent which funds 'had been paid over to final beneficiaries or was being held by intermediaries.'[6]

- there had been an overstatement of commitments due for payment, even when there was no longer any obligation to pay![7]

- there were weaknesses in the calculation of the final consequences (economic result) 'due to deficiencies in the Commission's accounting system'.[8]

As any accountant would know, if a set of accounts like these had been supplied by any company or corporation the board would have been investigated for malpractice, yet the EU's Commission managed to continue, being responsible for around £65 billion of European taxpayers' money.

Something is amiss

- Investigations threw up one case where a Mr François had been appointed to the Court of Auditors on a salary of around £6,000 a month. The problem was that Mr François was still claiming his pension from a former position in the Commission. Under the EU's own regulations he should not have been claiming both payments but apparently he was. Although this was brought to the attention of senior managers, no action was taken, apparently after the personal intervention of the Commission's President Jacques Delors.[9]

- Then there's the case of Mr Fasting whose organisation had been paid £635,000 by the EU for various reports until it was pointed out by Fasting that much of the report had been copied 'from his small son's geography atlas.'[10]

- There were two reports that had been commissioned from Mr Fasting over a period of four years, where much of the information in each report was identical. External auditors concluded that 'an unacceptably high incidence of "substantive" errors, which directly affected the amount or validity of the payments made.'[11]

- On other occasions, funds had been spent on such things as laptop computers, which were then passed back to staff within the departments for their own personal use. Of course, this money was allocated to projects outside the relevant departments but was being passed back to the same staff, who were managing the tenders.

- Then it was discovered that various EU staff were being paid twice for the same sets of expenses but even when this was uncovered, the money was never reclaimed.[12] Auditors found that 'There was little incentive for claimants not to overcharge, as there were no contractual penalties and no risk other than having to repay any amounts found to be overpaid.'[13]

Over time more accounting problems came to light.

- There existed a 'Leonardo da Vinci programme,' for vocational training and further training in the European Union. Here it was discovered that a £50,000 project had been awarded without any apparent open tendering.

In 1995 the EU commission had approved a policy initiative by a Mrs Edith Cresson (one of the EU's commissioners). This was intended for education and vocational training but came with a recommendation that the proposal be instigated regardless of costs. To complete the work a contract was being drawn up by a supposedly independent expert, Louise Recivieur, and the tender was eventually won by a Paris firm called Mayonic Public Relations.

When the details were checked it appeared that the Mayonic contract had been signed by the chairman of Mayonic, a Mrs Recivieur. Mrs Recivieur had, of course, been involved in drawing up the tender for her own company! What's more, Mrs Recivieur's firm had already been paid £180,000 by the EU. Finally, it was discovered that invoices had been paid for work that had not even been done.

The sums of money being allocated to the Leonardo project can only be described as alarming. Between '1995 to 2000, the estimated total cost was in the region of £400 million'[14] Eventually with the evidence reaching a point where it could not be ignored, the accounts were re-checked. What was found was a web of cover-ups and incompetence. The auditors were later to advise that the quality of the project had been 'remarkably low'. Even after the EU's own auditors had been highly critical of the project, senior managers still passed it for payment!

- Then, discrepancies in EU accounts were found amounting to around £450,000. What had been a surplus, had within a few pages had been marked in as a deficit, thereby mysteriously cancelling the amount out.

Rumours started to circulate that department records of accounts were being removed or lost. The exact same files that contained evidence relating to various financial discrepancies. Eventually, a letter was sent to 'Commissioner Gradin (anti-fraud), Comissioner Liikanen (budgets), Commissioner Van den Broek (out of courtesy) and Secretary-General Trojan,'[15] explaining what had been found. Incredibly, despite the warnings, the Commission then approved the next stage of Mrs Cresson's Leonardo programme. The total budget for the next stage of the project, Leonardo II was in the region of £2 billion - for the period 2000-04.

Is anyone listening?

Yet when the 626 members of the European Parliament (MEPs) were presented with the overwhelming evidence, only one MEP, Néllie Maes of the Vlaamse Volksunie, was prepared to take up the case. Even then it wasn't the EU that got to grips with the real extent of the cover-up but independent journalists who had suspicions that fraud was being carried out in the EU. Throughout 1998 the European Parliament withheld its accounts 'discharge' for the 1996 budget and, in January 1999, considered a motion of censure against the Commission. Then even more irregularities came to light -

- In the EU's special humanitarian aid section, ECHO, involving offshore companies and a commission official.

- In 1999 the BBC's current affairs programme Panorama screened an investigation that showed that the Russian Mafia had managed to set up EU front companies to claim EU subsidies![16]

Independent auditors concluded that 'a large proportion of the frauds detected in recent years have resulted from large-scale organised crime across national borders.'[17] The floodgates were opened... officials who were anxious about what they had found came forward. Eventually the seriousness of these allegations was so damning that the whole of the EU Commission resigned. As The Daily Telegraph newspaper reported:

> 'the European Union was thrown into the biggest crisis in its forty-two-year history last night, when the entire European Commission resigned following a damning report on corruption and nepotism inside the Brussels executive.'[18]

A 144-page report was commissioned by the EU by five independent 'wise men' and their criticisms were scathing. Although it absolved the 20 commissioners of direct involvement, it said that 'their claims to be unaware of undoubted instances of fraud and corruption, represented a serious admission of failure'.[19] It added that 'protestations of ignorance concerning problems that were often common knowledge in their services, even up to the highest levels, are tantamount to an admission of a loss of control by the political authorities over the administration they are supposedly running.' The main criticism of Jacques Santer, President of the European Commission at that time, was his failure to impose order on the Commission, which administers the EU's £65 billion-a-year budget.

After a debate lasting two days, the Parliament pulled back from censuring the Commission and instead voted to establish a

Committee of Independent Experts to examine specific allegations of fraud and mismanagement within the Commission.

What a mess!

Something had to be done, they needed someone to come in and clean the mess up, so the EU put Neil Kinnock in charge... The same Neil Kinnock who the British public had overwhelmingly failed to support in the general election in 1992... The same Neil Kinnock who in 1972 had voted against the UK joining the European Community.[20] Neil Kinnock was given 'overall responsibility for administration and reform in the Commission,'[21] essentially the task of cleaning up the EU's accounting systems and setting in place a system that would not allow more 'substantive errors.'

Mr Kinnock promised there was going to be 'root and branch reform'[22] but three years later the public were still waiting for all the answers when another whistle-blower came out of the cold. The European Commissions Chief Auditor Marta Andreasen met with Mr Kinnock to explain her concerns about the Commissions new accounting system, which seemed to be much like the old one!

She exposed a number of cases of fraud and mismanagement, including the lack of double accounting and 'glaring shortcomings' in the computer accounting system. This was not what anyone wanted to hear. She was suspended in August the same year.[23] Soon after this, the Commission's chief accountant was fired when she suggested to journalists that the EU budget was 'an open till waiting to be robbed.'

- Then by 2002 another scandal came to light whereby £3.5 million seems to have 'disappeared in slush funds and fictitious contracts,' relating to Eurostat, the agency within the EU that is supposed to keep a check on EU statistics (This is important as so much EU funding is allocated to projects based on these statistics!).

- The Luxembourg-based Eurostat organisation was suspected by EU anti-fraud investigators of illegitimately sub-contracting more than £1 million-worth of research work to Eurogramme, a London-based company run by a Mr Ojo, a former Commission employee.[24]

Anger at the EU

By 2002 some honest MEPS (and they do exist) who had still not seen any firm action were beginning to make their voices heard. The German MEP Gabriel Stauner complained that 'the climate was already reverting back to the bad old days'. She added, 'I am getting really angry. The Commission have lied to me about this case and I have the strong impression that they are trying to hide everything again.'[25] As Chris Heaton, a Conservative MEP in charge of scrutinising OLAF (another department that the EU has set up to fight fraud) said:

'The new anti-fraud office has been used as a dumping ground for compromised officials and is staffed at the top level by people accused of turning a blind eye to allegations in the 1990s.'

It seems to be that of the 92 cases that OLAF was supposed to be investigating for criminal activity, it has only pursued a prosecution in two cases.

So years on, is it now possible to say that the EU has finally sorted out its 'financial irregularities'? *Well in November 2003 for the ninth year in a row the EU's auditors refused to sign off their accounts!* Once all the errors were totted up it was estimated that of the total EU budget, 92 per cent was probably inaccurate. As one journalist pointed out:

> 'Imagine if we ran public companies, or even private societies on this basis. Picture the treasurer of say, your local golf club, announcing to the annual general meeting that, although he estimated that 8 per cent of the budget was stolen, it might be anything up to 92 per cent. Would you vote to pass his accounts? Would you want to keep him on as treasurer?'[26]

Conclusion

It seems increasingly clear that we will never know the true extent of the EU's financial problems. But as we move towards 2005, many European governments are preparing to sign up for an EU constitution and hand over even more money. *What, might we imagine, would the people of Europe say to this, if they were allowed to voice their true opinion?* Unfortunately, it is unlikely that they will ever be asked.

SECTION FIVE

PUBLIC AGENT 0207

The four men sat attentively in the smoke-filled room waiting for K to acknowledge their arrival. They had been summoned only minutes before as the emergency call sign had rung out across the surrounding buildings. K replaced the handset of the 330CB telephone on to its green Bakelite cradle, a soft, amber light burned for a moment, and then it faded. K looked up.

'Gentlemen, I'm afraid the situation is graver than we could have anticipated. We believe that a PEEDOFF agent has stolen the top-secret plans for the BSD-8001 prototype from a Russian Laboratory close to Syktyvkar.'

There was a gasp as the senior intelligence officers assessed the implications of the BSD-8001 falling into the hands of PEEDOFF.

K continued, ' The CIA picked up the same information via their satellites two hours ago and the President has asked for an immediate meeting of the joint intelligence staff. I have already spoken to President de Gaulle and Chancellor Adenauer of Germany, who has offered us every assistance in dealing with the threat.'

Johnson, London's head of counter-espionage asked, 'How much do we know about the BSD-8001?'

K pondered the question, then replied, 'I am afraid we know very little. Except that the BSD-8001 uses a thermal modification capacitor, to analyse speech patterns. It then interpolates them into various digital diffraction gratings before reassembling the structure and comparing for discrepancies, against an almost unlimited voice data bank. Gentlemen, our own scientists believe the BSD-8001 to be the most technologically advanced bullshit detector in existence.'

Harris, a humourless-looking Brylcreem'd lackey from the cabinet office, exclaimed, 'My god man, it could bring down the government.'

'We are aware of the gravity of the situation, which is why this afternoon I have dispatched our top agent, 0207, to Istanbul. Agent Bonk left some hours ago in the luggage hold of a BOAC jet. We believe the handover will take place tonight around 8pm local time. That is all the information we have,' K replied.

The telescopic lens of the 7.62mm SVD Dragunov sniper rifle steadied on the two targets. The handover was to take place in a park close to Taya Hutun Street between a luckless PEEDOFF agent and an unknown courier. They had both been double-crossed. Iana Hislopoff, the mastermind behind PEED-OFF had planned to kill them both and make it appear that the Russians had retrieved their stolen machine. The £25 million handover fee would be a bonus.

The PEEDOFF assassin steadied his aim and levelled his finger on the hair trigger. Without warning, Bonk suddenly stepped forward out of nowhere and struck the assassin a fatal karate blow to the medulla oblongata. He slumped to the ground.

'Sorry, it's not your day old man,' said Bonk nonchalantly. Bonk picked up the rifle and re-aimed through the PSO-1 optical sight. In the half-light he could see the PEEDOFF agent and a courier exchanging attaché cases. Bonk took aim and fired a high velocity round through the PEEDOFF agent's forehead. He then turned the gun towards the courier. The courier ran screaming in sheer panic. Enough killing for one day thought Bonk and instead he sent a warning shot past the man's ear as he disappeared into the darkness.

Bonk could not condone gratuitous violence. He only did what was necessary to get the job done. He pulled out his handgun and slowly crossed the park, checking for any assassins that he might have missed. He stopped and carefully opened the two attaché cases. In one he found the BSD-8001 prototype. It looked like a small metal box with four delicate crystal valves and in the other attaché case he found bundles of cash. He put the BSD-8001 into his pocket and picked up the other attaché case. By now he could hear police sirens wailing in the distance.

Bonk casually walked out of the park and along the road, deliberately avoiding the grim streetlights that bathed the street in a sickly hue of sodium orange. He stopped at a kiosk to confirm that nobody was following him and bought a late edition of *Zaman* along with a pack of high-tar cigarettes before walking on. The newspaper would be good cover to help blend in with the locals. The plan was to make his way overland to

Izmir and once he neared there to pick up further instructions at a dead-letter drop.

Three miles South of Izmir he stopped and gazed at the beautiful turquoise of the Mediterranean, falling away across the horizon. Any other time it would have been good to find a local bar and have breakfast but Bonk had work to do. He took a small compass from the heel of his shoe and rechecked his coordinates carefully skirting along the beach. Stopping at a small palm tree, he walked thirty yards southwest, then stopped. He moved back three large stones. Underneath, he found an army-issue rucksack. He opened it and could see it contained instructions and some objects wrapped in brown paper. He read the note.

'0207, you have made it this far. I have enclosed a few gadgets for you. A box of flammable matches, an inflatable mini-submarine, a bar of chocolate made of soap and some second-class stamps. Sorry, it's not much but with Treasury cutbacks you were lucky to get these.

Best wishes, K.

PS don't waste the stamps'.

For the next hour, Bonk sat on the beach inflating the submarine. I really ought to give up smoking he thought. When it was ready he emptied the money into the rucksack and buried the attaché case. He carried the inflatable submarine down to the water's edge and climbed in.

Ten days later, Bonk's mini-submersible bobbed to the surface of Pen B of Chatham dockyard. The surprised guards immediately took him into custody, until he was able to confirm that he was he, in fact, Commander Bonk of the Royal Navy. After a mug of cocoa with a shot of rum, he was escorted to a military vehicle ready and waiting to whisk him away.

The driver sarcastically said, 'We don't get many agents arriving in Chatham.'

Bonk didn't reply. Twenty miles down the A2 road heading back towards London, the driver turned to Bonk and pulled out a small Luger pistol from inside his jacket pocket.

'Empty the contents of the rucksack on to the dashboard, this is where you get out, 0207,' the driver smirked.

Bonk did as instructed and emptied the contents of the rucksack on to the dashboard.

'Yes that's right, I work for PEEDOFF. You *Bweetesh* think you are so clever but you are all fools.'

Bonk just stared ahead, a cold look in his eye.

'Give me that chocolate,' said the driver, 'I'm hungry.'
Bonk pushed it slowly towards the driver. With one hand on the wheel the PEEDOFF agent put the gun down and broke off a piece of chocolate. He ate it greedily. 'Russian chocolate is better,' he said, as bubbles started to foam out of his mouth and he started to cough. Bonk saw his chance. He leaned over, opened the driver's door and pushed the driver out of the moving vehicle. With a bang, he pulled the door shut and pressed his foot hard on to the accelerator.

By the early morning, he had abandoned the vehicle close to Embankment tube station and made his way towards the forbidding M16 building.

'Good morning, Commander Bonk,' said the guard. 'We were

expecting you back yesterday, sir.'

Bonk made his way up to the fifth floor, the rucksack in hand. As he went into the briefing room he could see K sitting at the head of a long mahogany table. Johnson and Harris were sitting next to him, discussing some blueprints that were laid out on the table.

'Bonk! About time, we've been waiting here for you. Have you got the BSD-8001?' said K.

'It's in the rucksack,' said Bonk, as he carefully placed the rucksack on the table.

Suddenly, Johnson pulled a Colt 45 revolver from his pocket. He then pulled the rucksack towards himself.

'Johnson,' said Harris, surprised at this new turn of events.

'He's working freelance for Hislopoff, he's been promised a senior job within PEEDOFF,' said Bonk.

'I knew Johnson was full of bullshit, as soon as I arrived, sir,' said Bonk.

'Why did you do it Johnson?' asked K.

'Why should I wait for a measly pension, when the BSD-8001 is worth zillions of roubles? You and your public intelligence service. It's just a big joke,' said Johnson.

Bonk sat down,' You don't mind if I have a cigarette old chap?'

He took out a crumpled pack of Camel full strength and the matches from his top pocket

'Go ahead it will be your last,' said Johnson.

As Bonk lit the match, a plume of blue smoke filled the room. A gunshot rang out. When the smoke had cleared Johnson lay dead, slumped over the table. A neat bullet hole through his temple.

'Good heavens, I wouldn't have believed it of Johnson, he seemed so loyal.' said K. 'It's good to have a man like you on our side, Bonk'

Bonk pulled of his felt hat and strands of golden hair fell down.

'I don't believe it,' said Harris, 'you're a woman. I mean you're a really sexy curvaceous women.'

'Yes I am a woman. My real name is Jane Bonk. In this profession it's dangerous to make assumptions. I took the liberty of switching the BSD-8001 on my way back from Chatham. The real one is in my pocket.'

'You will be put on a charge for this Bonk,' said K.

'Send it to my tailor. I have an appointment there in one hour. There's nothing like shopping to relax after a rough day.' Bonk turned on her heels and left the room.

'Bonk seems to have got a bit above herself' intoned Harris,

'Thank goodness, the whole sorry saga is over and we are still in control of the situation,' said K.

'I completely agree, Harris. Gentlemen, shall we get on with today's business? I have here the blueprints outlining proposals for the new office biscuit, I think we can all agree that milk chocolate coated biscuits are best?'

Chapter Eleven

✔

Direct Democracy Discussion Forum

There are two main ways that direct democracy initiatives might be discussed with the public. The first is with specific questions put to the electorate in a referendum. The second would be with questionnaires containing detailed policy proposals. For example a direct democracy candidate might propose the measures below (with a guarantee that only those policies that the public supported would be implemented once in power). This would be rather than producing vaguely worded political manifestos that are rarely followed. At the end of each proposal, you would be asked whether or not you would like to support the measure (much like on a questionnaire).

Health

Most of us would like to believe that when money is allocated to Britain's health service most of it reaches the patient. In reality, as New Labour has discovered, much of this money disappears down a bureaucratic black hole. So what exactly happens to it all? We start with the politicians who advise Her Majesty's Treasury to collect as much money as it can. This task is passed on to the Inland Revenue and the Customs and Excise, who enthusiastically collect it (while taking a cut). The money is passed back to the Treasury (who take a cut)… who pass it to the Department of Health (who take a very substantial cut)… who pass it via various quangos (who take quite a bit more)... who agree that it should be passed to the larger Health Authorities (who take another considerable slice)... who then pass it to the Primary Care Trust managers (who need their share)... who pass it to the local care units (whose managers have to be paid)... who pass it to their sub-managers (who also need to be paid)... who eventually pass it to the doctors and nurses to treat patients!

Even though they already have too much work to do, the same doctors and nurses have to account for every minute allocated, every penny spent, and each prescription they write out, by filling in efficiency forms, target projections, attending management meetings and confirming that all new administrative directives have been put into place. Is it any wonder that the morale of doctors and nurses, who are trying to run an efficient health service, is at an all-time low? This is borne out by record number of GPs, consultants and experienced nurses who are retiring early or simply leaving the health service.

At the present time, the British National Health Service (NHS) is collapsing under the weight of supporting a plethora of managers, administrators, non-departmental public bodies, quangos, commissioners, innumerable regulators and a multitude of inspectors. All of which adds to the cost of the NHS, and leaves doctors and nurses to deal with the bureaucratic deluge it creates. As an example, in March 2004, The Times newspaper reported that an NHS *'efficiency unit'* had wasted £70,000 after repeatedly cancelling conferences at the executive Belfry Hotel near Birmingham! An NHS spokesman later confirmed the article.[1]

New Labour's answer to these concerns was to set doctors more targets and allocate more funds to various administrative bodies - including over 70 health quangos. Many of these quangos now have a remit beyond the supervision of Parliament, while controlling vast amounts of taxpayers' money. One example is the National Institute for Clinical Excellence. In reality, a quango. The National Institute for Clinical Excellence draws up guidelines as to what drugs or treatments can be used within hospitals but includes representatives of pharmaceutical corporations. Their decisions are difficult to scrutinise because they hold meetings in private.[2]

Is there a better way?

There is a sensible and practical alternative, as was discussed in Douglas Carswell's book, Direct Democracy. Health service funding could be passed directly from the Treasury to locally elected County Health Directors, who would be responsible for their own regions. For counties that had a population of less than one million, one director might have responsibility for a group of surrounding counties. Funding would be allocated under a formula that took into account, population size, demographics and geography. For instance some areas have a higher percentage of older people or children. Some areas have a relatively small population, dispersed over a larger geographic area.

Politicians would decide the amount allocated to the total National Health Budget but they would not be allowed to micro-manage how the money was being spent. To explain in more detail what would happen, let me give you a scenario for the County of Durham. A local person with medical and managerial experience would be elected by the local people to be become the County Health Director of Durham. Their term of office would last four years before they would have to stand for re-election.

There would be strict rules that the director in office could not use public money to fund a re-election campaign. Anyone who had been a member of any political party in the previous five years would be excluded from applying to the position, as would senior executives of outside suppliers or contractors. If the County Health Director achieved the required results over the four years, it would be for local people to decide if they wanted him/her to continue.

The County Health Director of Durham would have complete control over the budget (regularly audited by independent auditors), deciding locally what health services needed to be made available. Durham's County Director would have the freedom to buy in services from other areas. For instance, he/she might find that Lincolnshire Health Trust is more able to deal with a backlog of hip operations. Durham could buy in services from Lincolnshire to reduce the waiting list. Alternatively, Durham's Health Director might decide to bring in extra teams of consultant surgeons for a limited period. Health Directors would be free to use the private sector, if they could negotiate a more cost-effective price but this would not be compulsory.

The Director and his/her staff would decide what equipment was needed, what drugs were required and what needed spending on maintenance to their building, etc. If they so wished they could join together with other trusts to negotiate better prices for drugs and services. They would also determine local salaries for doctors, GPs and nurses (if local GPs and nurses chose to remain outside the national pay scheme). The Department of Health would be substantially reduced in size and kept as a facility for information for the access of the County Health Trusts, their directors, doctors, consultants and nurses.

The position of County Health Director would have a salary commensurate to the size of the county and local costs. Each County Health Director would a set budget but they could not spend more than a specified percentage on their own department's administration. They would have a board of local independent governors, whose job it would be to check audits, compare costs for products and facilities, and publish their findings at the end of each year. Accounts would be freely available to the public at all times. Decisions on finance above specified costings would have to be supported by the board. The board would also be elected locally (again restricting members of political parties to a maximum of 25 per cent).

All of this would have a variety of knock-on effects.

- It would free up a substantial amount of money that is presently wasted on unnecessary bureaucracy.

- It would allow local Health Trusts to be more innovative and deal more quickly with local problems.

- Health Directors would be able to purchase resources at the most effective price and best value.

- Local services would be accountable to local people and accounting systems would be transparent.

- The public would be able to compare results from one area to another and share experience in solving different healthcare issues.

- It would sidestep the yearly squabbles that take place between the present political parties, as it would be the County Health Director who was responsible to local people.

- The health service would remain in public ownership but have an obligation to find the most cost-effective solution.

- It would substantially reduce the amount of paperwork that doctors and nurses have to do.

Is there any indication that the public would respond well to local people running local services? Certainly at the last general election, Dr Richard Taylor became an independent MP for Wyre Forest, campaigning to keep Kidderminster Hospital's accident and emergency department open. He trounced the major political parties by gaining 60 per cent of the local vote.

Would you like to see these proposals on health introduced?

> *Please tick one:*
> ( ) *Yes*
> ( ) *No*
> ( ) *I would like more information*

Dentists

In February 2004 in Queen Street, Scarborough, a queue of people appeared outside a new dentist surgery.[3] The reason was that it was the first new NHS (national health service) dental surgery to open in the area in eight years. Most dentists are private, not from lack of NHS fees but because of the NHS bureaucracy that they have to deal with. We have to look at ways of reducing the amount of paperwork otherwise we will soon have no NHS dentists left!

There might also be a case for the government to offer to pay for dental students' education in return for agreeing to work for the national health service for at least ten years. They could either choose to fund themselves or take the grants and work for a set period thus increasing the number of NHS dentists.

Why is it that GPs are paid according to how many patients they have on their records, while NHS dentists are paid by how many cavitys they fill? We might amend the system of payment so that dentists are also paid for how many patients they have registered with them. This would encourage dentists to emphasise the benefits of preventative care rather than be paid for the amount of treatment they undertake.

When treatment takes place, the NHS already subsidises the cost of the drugs and equipment and we would not envisage this changing. We might also make available a capital fund that dentists can use to buy new equipment. It is surprising to see how many dentists in the UK are still using techniques that are becoming increasingly obsolete elsewhere. In the United States it is now common for dentists to use lasers rather than drills, which although more expensive are far more comfortable for the patient. We would like to see a capital investment fund set up whereby NHS dentists can apply to the fund for low interest loans to update equipment.

Would you like to see these proposals on dentistry introduced?

Please tick one:

( ) Yes

( ) No

( ) I would like more information

Education – five plus five equals six

Many parents in Britain can only dream that their children were educated in schools that had the same facilities as an average independent day-school. With fees for 'private day-schools' at around £5,000, this is well beyond the means of most parents. What many parents don't realise is that at the present time, each child in state education in Britain is already allocated around £4,600 a year and according to the Chancellor of the Exchequer's own figures this will to rise to £4,900 a year by 2005/6.[4] The quality of British State schools does not reflect this, because so much of the £41,984 million education budget is spent on bureaucracy, long before it reaches the classroom.

So where does the money go? The Department for Education and Skills (DfES) and the Local Education Authorities spend around £11,515 million.[5] You then have various quangos, including the Qualifications and Curriculum Authority, who spend around £60 million and the Teacher Training Agency, who take another £392 million (which had risen to £425 million by 2003).[6] The money is further reduced when it goes via local councils, who decide what percentage of the education budget is to be spent on education (they are, in fact, entitled to spend it on services unrelated to education!). The remainder is then passed to the Local Education Authorities (LEAs) who produce what is termed the Individual Schools Budget. Only then are local schools allocated individual funds with which they are forced to buy supplies and equipment via government departments, that is often more expensive than if purchased locally. You couldn't devise a more tortuous route if you locked up ten quangos in a classroom for a week!

Unbeknown to most parents, a few more organisations take their cut. In 1998 following the introduction of the national curriculum, the National Curriculum Council was set up. In 1988 its annual budget was around £10 million. It has now risen to £60 million employing around 460 staff.[7] The New Learning and Skills Council, which funds education for over 16s, comprises a national body and 47 local councils. It managed to appoint 800 senior staff before it had even started operating![8] In 2003-04 OFSTED's budget was £197 million, an increase equivalent to 36 per cent every year since its inception just over ten years ago.[9]

It all adds up

There is now so much educational administration and vested interest at work, that no government has ever dared to challenge it. Our proposal is to make all state schools, colleges and universities non-

181

profit making educational trusts. Politicians would agree a total education budget but would not be able to interfere in the day-to-day running of classes. It would be left up to head teachers, governors, teachers and parents to achieve the required standards. Head teachers would be given control over their own budgets and assets, with careful auditing checks put in place as with the Health Trusts. Each School Trust would comprise head teachers and a board of governors, elected by the school's parents (with parents making up fifty per cent of the numbers).

The school would be free to purchase materials, services, extra staff or catering from wherever they could get the best value for money. Each school budget would be decided using a formula that would take into account the amount of pupils, its geographic location, the type of school and the demographics of an area. The number of administration staff would depend on the number of pupils attending the school. It would be the school's responsibility to negotiate rates of pay with their staff and teachers, who could either stay in or opt out of a national pay scheme. This would put the status of teachers on to a more professional level and avoid yearly disputes with the government.

Head teachers' salaries would have an upper limit that also took into account the size of the school. Teachers would, of course, be free to choose whether or not they wished to remain with their unions. Schools could choose whether or not to specialise in certain areas, such as maths, science, art, technology, special needs, sports or even fashion and theatre. All centrally controlled targets and guidelines such as the national curriculum would be abolished. It would be for the head teachers, governors and parents to agree on targets. And academic results would be published yearly.

All this would open the way for the funding of home schools, which in many deprived areas have become an increasingly popular and successful way to educate children. Those who would most benefit would be parents whose children have no option but to go to poorly funded state schools, with low standards and low aspirations. New schools could be set up if there was enough demand in the local area and if the proposed head teacher could gain enough local support. There would be a government capital fund that would be allocated on merit. It would also be made illegal for the trusts or local councils to sell off any land or playing fields attached to the school. The sale of land belonging to schools has caused many problems, depriving a lot of children of outdoor areas for games.

Setting boundaries

Many schools now have severe discipline problems but by involving parents more closely in all aspects of schooling, schools might be in a better position to address these problems. Teachers describe how some difficult pupils are intent on ruining other pupils' education with disruptive behaviour. Schools should be able set their own discipline practices within the law but outside of government interference. We also need to legislate over teachers' responsibilities more clearly. At the present time, teachers are not even sure if they are legally allowed to stop bullying without concerns that they will be sued. Teachers' liability should be clarified within sensible limits.

The DfES would become a much smaller resource, offering guidance when requested from schools and incorporating teacher training qualifications and OFSTED inspections, but the DfES would lose the right to interfere to the extent that it does now. Between 1997 and 2001, schools were sent over 1000 publications and sets of regulations from the Department of Education, including 140 guidance documents to teachers during a six-month period alone.[10] This is absurd, not least because teachers do not have the time to read so much extra paperwork!

A clause in the school trust's remit would state that the school is run for the benefit of the children as a non-profit making educational organisation. Schools would have control over their own admissions procedures and exclusions. The DfES would be able to keep a check on schools and would be able to issue warning to governors if a school was falling below standard. In such cases, the school would be taken under the wing of the inspectors until a new administration could be found.

LEAs would have to be self-sustaining as they would not receive any direct subsidies, supplying services to schools such as insurance, school materials, temporary staff; and legal services. In the event of a school trust going bankrupt, the school would not be handed back to the government but sold for a nominal sum to a new administration. Liability would be covered by the trust's own insurance scheme. The Transfer and Undertaking of Employment Law would be transferred to the new governors.

The same principle could also be applied to colleges of higher education and universities, where the university board of governors would include student representation. As students pay more and more for their education, they should also have more control in how money is allocated. Universities would be given more freedom to spend their budgets in the way they think most suitable.

Would you like to see these proposals on education introduced? Please tick one:

> *Please tick one:*
> *( ) Yes*
> *( ) No*
> *( ) I would like more information*

Law and order

In the last twenty years crime figures have doubled in the UK, while politicians seem incapable of taking effective action. A great deal of money that could be allocated to frontline services is now spent on reports, guidelines, targets and management efficiency schemes. Both the police and the Crown Prosecution Service (CPS) have become less accountable to the public as more quangos, such as the Police Standards Unit have been introduced by successive governments. One complaint from policemen on the beat is that they are spending more time filling in forms than policing.

An alternative would be to have elected County Chief Constables, under the remit of Parliamentry Law but who are, at the same time, accountable to the local electorate. These Chief Constables would receive their own budgets direct from the Treasury and be accountable to a board of local governors. The governors would include locally elected people and the Chief Constable's term of office would last for four years. Whether they were re-elected would depend on the quality of service that they had provided and the votes of local people. The same auditing rules that would apply for schools and hospitals would apply.

If let's say, the County Police Constable for Cheshire decided that he/she wanted to instigate a zero-tolerance policy towards local crime, his/her team would be free to do so. Responsibility for prosecuting criminals would be handed directly to the County Chief Constable who could take advice from his own prosecuting team. It would be his/her decision to allocate money to staff, training, equipment or vehicles, as well as decided what percentage of the money should be used for community projects. We have seen a tendency for local forces to be forced into spending more and more time on community action projects. In some cases these have yielded results but in many cases, they have been nothing more than a public relations exercise for politicians.

The police should be free to carry out their duties and have the support of our judiciary, which is collapsing under too much bureaucracy. We should disband the CPS and incorporate it into the County Chief Constable's remit. Since the CPS was started in 1985, there are now 65 per cent fewer convictions among 14- to 18-year-olds than in 1984, yet the number of crimes committed by underaged criminals has soared.[11] Alcohol abuse and related crimes alone, are estimated to be costing the country in the region of £25 billion pounds a year, and this estimate does not take into account the psychological cost to road accident victims and secondary victims such as the families of those affected.[12]

Total crime figures

According to the government's own figures, crime in the UK has risen dramatically. In 1950 the amount of crimes officially recorded was just under half a million, by 2003 it stood at over 5 million![13] With the emphasis on determining whether a prosecution is in the 'public's interest' and an eye to criminal (political) statistics, the number of criminals cautioned rather than prosecuted has increased dramatically. At the same time, the amount of unsolved crimes has increased.

It is no wonder that many people have stopped reporting minor crimes because in many cases they feel it is a waste of time. A policy of zero tolerance - when supported with enough funding, a reduction in bureaucracy and the restriction of government interference - can be highly effective. One of the most influential exponent's of the policy of zero tolerance was Rudy Giuliani, who was elected mayor of New York in 1993. In that same year, the murder rate in

New York dropped by 19 per cent, the biggest fall in New York's history.[14] There was also a drop of 67,000 in the total amount of crimes recorded across the whole of the United States. What is incredible is that 41,000 of this total was due to New York alone! Over the same period, 400,000 less people were claiming welfare benefits as a reinvigorated New York employed more people.[15]

During the seventies, although New York was a vibrant city, it was not a safe city. Drugs were being sold openly on the streets, there was vandalism of almost every public amenity, there was graffiti everywhere and nuisance begging at every road junction and cash point. At night-time local people avoided much of the city, and those who did venture out became easy targets for criminals. The atmosphere was one of fear. As Andrew Kirtzman described:

> 'It is hard to state the degree to which the culture of the city changed under Mayor Giuliani. New Yorkers walking to work no longer encountered men urinating on the sidewalk. They no longer travelled in graffiti-covered trains... They didn't fear for their safety as they exited on to deserted streets... and old ladies in the park no longer talked about who'd been mugged over the weekend.'[16]

Today, New York is full of life, clean and safe, with a genuine feeling of community and a sense that the city is making progress. With a proliferation of cafes, open-air concerts, festivals, markets and street galleries, it feels like a good place to be. Over the same 25-year period, the reverse has occurred in London. The streets are strewn with litter, there's graffiti everywhere, vandalism is part of everyday life and there are some parts of London that have now become no-go areas for pedestrians. There is a sense that London is somewhere you have to pass through, to get to somewhere else. But London is not alone in having a serious crime problem. Parts of Birmingham, Manchester, Liverpool and Edinburgh face similar problems together with many large cities across Europe. Something needs to change, and leaving the running of the police force to unaccountable committees is not the answer. Control needs to be given back to local people and their communities.

Gun Crime

We also need to address the alarming rise in gun crime. In London there is now so much money being made from the sale of drugs that guns have become fashion accessories. In the UK in 1977, there were around 100 acts of violence involving firearms. By 1999 the figure had risen to 600.[17] It is the criminal's choice to carry a gun and they need to understand that it will not be tolerated. In our model of direct democracy we would propose adding a mandatory tariff of fifteen years without parole for any crime involving firearms.

As Mayor Giuliani discovered in New York, it doesn't take long for word to get around that violent criminals are being targeted. The UK still have a choice: it can act soon or face a future in which the police will have to be armed and the streets will be less tolerable. We would also propose a heavy increase in the penalties for gun smuggling, raising the sentence to twenty years without probation. This particular problem is a European one, as there are now many illegal guns available because of major conflicts around the world, but the public ought to have the right to feel safe in their communities.

Would you like to see these proposals on law and order introduced?

Please tick one:

        ( ) *Yes*

        ( ) *No*

        ( ) *I would like more information*

Asylum and Immigration

Although a heated debate has taken place between the major political parties in the UK over asylum and immigration, it has been rather disingenuous. *The reason being that British politicians handed over control of UK immigration policy to a variety of international bodies including the European Union.* This means that even though the issue of immigration is debated, British politicians have little control over immigration legislation.

In 1951 Britain signed up to the United Nation's Convention on Refugees, which at present obliges all UK governments to offer asylum to 'anybody claiming' to be persecuted. This means that the UK has to allow refugees into the country and claims can only be validated once applicants have arrived. The British government incorporated this into British law with the passing of the 1996 Asylum and Immigration Act. For an asylum seeker to be removed, the British government now has the legal obligation to prove that an application is 'manifestly unfounded'.

Incredibly, Britain's own judiciary interpreted the United Nations Convention on Refugees to mean that France and Germany could not be deemed as safe countries![18] With permeable borders across Europe, what this has meant is that refugees can travel across Europe, through France into the UK but cannot be returned legally via France. During 1999 of 21,200 asylum applicants who were refused asylum in the UK, approximately 75% remained in Britain.[19] Mr. Blunkett, Britain's Home Secretary even admitted, that the government did not have accurate figures for how many illegal immigrants were now resident in the UK.

In 1999, 100,000 people were officially accepted for resettlement into the UK. This is the equivalent to an annual population increase of approximately 0.17 per cent.[20] In March 2004 Steve Moxon, who worked for the Immigration and Nationality Directorate, was suspended from his job after he revealed to the media that his department was manipulating immigration figures to put them in a better light. He said, 'his unit was told to waive key checks on applications from certain nationals of the ten states due to join the European Union on 1 May 2004.'[21]

Now that the European Convention on Human Rights has been incorporated into UK law, even more pressure has been put on the UK's welfare system. EU law supersedes UK sovereignty on these issues, so the UK can be heavily fined if these regulations are not adhered to. Because of a democratic loophole, representatives, primarily from the Foreign Office, have negotiated these agreements without the approval of Parliament or the electorate.

If we look back over the history of Britain we can see that many refugees have arrived in the UK from all over the world, and many have contributed to Britain's economy, traditions and character. But with the ten new EU countries of Eastern Europe there are potentially 74 million people who have the right to move to Britain looking for work. After talking tough, the government declared that they would not *initially* be allowed welfare benefits!

Illegal Work Gangs

In Morecombe Bay, Lancashire, on the night of 6 February 2004, nineteen illegal Chinese workers tragically drowned after being caught in a night tide while picking cockles. Most of them had been working illegally for local criminal gangs. Illegal immigration also has implications for national security, with the government itself admitting that, of course, it doesn't know who has entered the country illegally. So what affect does this have? There has always been immigration to Britain but these changes took place relatively slowly. What we have seen in the last twenty years is an acceleration of the introduction of new cultural norms, that on occasions have been highly insensitive to the wishes of the indigenous British people. We may abhor racism, but why should a country half the size of France be expected to have a moral obligation to take in proportionally more immigrants than any other European country?

What the UK needs is a period of stability. Further proposals might include:

- A system similar to the USA, where Green Cards are available for a period before full citizenship is offered. During a period of five years, if the applicant is prosecuted for a serious criminal offence, they would be returned to their country of origin.

- Green cards would be refused to anybody who had been shown to have a criminal record, wherever the crimes were committed.

- Illegal immigrants and failed asylum seekers would be returned to their country of origin.

- Restricting the time frame that relatives can be brought into the country on the back of new citizenship. This would mean that only once the applicant had cleared the five year period, then another two years as a citizen, would other members of an applicant's family (other than dependent children) be allowed into the UK.

- Various loopholes that exist to foreign nationals overstaying educational visas should be closed and severe fines put in place for the directors of company's who employ people without the necessary work permits.

- The UK could allow those into the country as in the US who are prepared to invest a minimum sum of £100,000 into a business while applying for citizenship. It would have to be proven that this is new money that has not simply been diverted out of the UK.

- Any person who has been found to attempt to enter the UK illegally, would be permanently banned from applying for citizenship or entering the country again.

- Eye-scanning and fingerprint checking could be introduced on all passports to reduce the amount of fraudulent attempts used to circumvent immigration controls.

- Fast tracking could take place for certain applicants who showed a minimum qualification of a recognise degree in specific subjects deemed to be helpful. Such as electronics, medicine or nursing qualifications. (Although not deliberately approach developing countries who themselves were suffering shortages of skilled staff in these areas).

- All Green card applicants would be expected to take an oath to uphold the law of their destination country and not become involved in illegal activities.

- Passport applications would include a basic spoken and written test.

- Visas requirements to enter the UK could be made more stringent and if necessary Visas would be refused to countries that have shown to have lax control systems. Incredibly, there are some countries which are known to allow illegals to travel to the United Kingdom, where the only requirement is that they hold a return air ticket, for entry into the UK!

- That all visitors to the UK have compulsory medical insurance cover for the period of their stay. (This is a proposal to reduce the amount of Health Tourists whose sole purpose of visiting the UK is to use NHS facilities). Insurance would have to cover the length of visa stay and be available to visitors at cost, when they arrive in the UK if they had not already arranged suitable cover in their country of origin.

- Green card entitlement would not give an automatic right to citizenship. It could be withdrawn at any time, if the rules and regulations regarding entitlement were transgressed.

Would you like to see these proposals on immigration introduced?   Please tick one:

> ( ) *Yes*
> ( ) *No*
> ( ) *I would like more information*

Community Charge

As discussed earlier, in our system of direct democracy there would be changes to the way education and the police are funded, which would, in effect, reduce the role of local councils. We would propose to limit the amount that Community Charge could rise by pegging it to the government's official rate of inflation. There is little to justify Community Charge rising year on year by as much as 20 per cent, while wages and pensions remain linked to inflation.

Would you like to see these proposals on local Community Charge introduced?

Please tick one:
( ) *Yes*
( ) *No*
( ) *I would like more information*

Pensions

Recent years have seen a variety of scandals involving company pension schemes. What is interesting is that we can look back and see how the government handled the predicted crisis. As one writer wrote:

> 'The disturbing thing about re-reading the committee minutes afterwards is the accuracy with which MPs pointed the key flaw was in the legislation - the lack of proper protections against high pressure salesmen, the opacity of the all-important information about how much of the pension holder's money would be swallowed up by commissions and administrative costs, pocketed by the companies, the danger of innocent people being bilked. All were preventable. What was predicted, then happened. In some cases the government, to limit the damage that followed later, adopted the very proposals, which were laughed at by ministers,'[22]

Although, retrospectively, some steps have been taken to help the situation, there are others that could make a difference such as:

- Making it a statutory requirement that all private pension assets are held and controlled by a board of governors elected by the pension contributors.

- Ensuring that accounts are available at all times for scrutiny by pension contributors.

- Making sure that all hidden costs are available for scrutiny by pension holders.

- Keeping the assets out of reach of company directors.

- Allowing for a majority vote of pension holders to move or put on hold the scheme at any time.

- Ensuring that more severe penalties are in place for administrators who break the regulations.

Some of these measures are in the process of being put into place but there is one aspect of that has not been addressed.

Pension audit trails should be made more visible and easier to access. Around two thirds of pensions are invested in the stock market yet very few people with pensions have any idea of where their funds are. By having access to an internet-based information service that has to be updated every month, people would be able to see where their money has been invested. This would not only give the public an opportunity to see what is being done on their behalf but also gauge how well funds are doing.

Would you like to see these proposals on pensions introduced?

Please tick one:

( ) Yes

( ) No

( ) I would like more information

Profit sharing

In our system of direct democracy we would also introduce universal profit sharing as a statutory requirement for all companies with over 100 staff. A percentage of the company's profit would be shared out equally between all staff, with the percentage being set by government legislation. The intention with this proposal is to allow staff to share in the profitability of their companies and give them an incentive other than their salary.

In companies where this has been applied it has often increased productivity and reduced the inherent tensions between staff and managers, as every one unites towards the same goal of the company becoming more profitable. The rate might be set at (say) 10 per cent of a company's annual dividend, to be shared equally between all staff that have been with the company for at least one year.

Company directors already have an obligation to consider shareholders when sharing dividends. It doesn't seem unreasonable that they consider their main stakeholders (i.e. their staff and employees), who are as an important an asset as any other. This would be a scheme that would benefit all employees, from the chief executive to the cleaning staff.

Would you like to see these proposals on profit sharing
introduced?   *Please tick one:*

             ( ) *Yes*
             ( ) *No*
             ( ) *I would like more information*

Shareholders

We would also like to see legislation introduced that permits shareholders to have more control over directors' bonuses, pension schemes and dividends linked to performance. Over recent years we have see some appalling examples of corporate greed whereby directors of financially failing companies have paid themselves huge rewards with no justification.

At the present time, there is far too many examples of directors making decisions about each others bonuses, which means that they, of course, have a vested interest in being as generous to each other as possible, with little regard to shareholders or employees.

Would you like to see these proposals on shareholders' rights introduced?   Please tick one:

    ( ) *Yes*

    ( ) *No*

    ( ) *I would like more information*

Small businesses

We are also proposing a series of tax concessions for small business-es that can show that they receive 70 per cent, or more of their income from local companies. This would benefit local businesses such as smaller shops and employees who help the local economy. The problem with relying on large corporations is that the money spent by local people is too often moved away from the area, only widening the gap between commerce and the local community.

We might also initiate a proposal to help small businesses, which would mean banks had to clear funds for businesses and personal account holders within 48 hours. Most of the largest banks are able to clear their own funds within 24 hours, if not sooner, and no con-vincing explanation has ever been given why banks can hold over funds at the customer's expense.

Would you like to see these proposals to help small businesses
introduced?   Please tick one:

    ( ) *Yes*

    ( ) *No*

    ( ) *I would like more information*

Innovation courses

We would also like to propose the setting up of Innovation Courses at universities and colleges, which would incorporate product design, engineering skills marketing, but most importantly invent-ing. Individuals in the UK patent around 20,000 new ideas every year, but only 2 per cent of them are ever marketed. Britain has had a long tradition of innovation but this has been stifled by the cost of patenting law, which makes it unrealistic for many small business to produce their own products.

There are some organisations that have begun to address this, such as the Nesta organisation,[23] which offers grants via the lottery fund. There are also a variety of smaller organisations offering advice on patenting and innovation but one website offering all this information would be would be helpful. We would also like schools to start offering innovation courses. It would be a cross between design and innovation technology, with the emphasis on the process of invention, plus mechanical and practical skills.

Would you like to see these proposals for innovation courses introduced? Please tick one:

    ( ) Yes
    ( ) No
    ( ) I would like more information

The fishing industry

One of the industries that have been irrevocably damaged by government mismanagement is the UK's fishing industry. As an example, the city of Hull at one time had the biggest fishing industry in Europe. Now there are only a tiny fraction of the fishing boats left. As Peregrine Worsthorne said:

'Telling the truth about the reasons for Britain's fishing policy, for example, would almost certainly involve telling Parliament a murky story which any self respecting minister would rather not tell; and, if told would cause one hell of a stink. In short, the myth of parliamentary sovereignty would not long survive if ministers always told the truth. So perhaps it is a mercy that even the best of them do not do so.'[24]

Our intention would be to reinstate the UK's 200 mile fishing zone and set aside 36 per cent of this area as a conservation zone, covering areas that are known to be spawning grounds for young fish stocks. This would still be an improvement on the situation now but would allow stocks to recover to sustainable levels. We would also propose to:

- Set aside a 30-mile coastal zone specifically for coastal fleets.

- A six-mile coastal belt would be locally managed.

- Foreign fishing vessels would only be allowed into the UK's zone under strict licence conditions and industrial fishing fleets would be severely limited.

- We should switch to a 'days at sea quota' for stocks where fishermen are allowed to keep all that they catch in a set period but are restricted to which days they can fish, rather than the wasteful system we have now, where unwanted species are thrown overboard as dead waste (if fishermen catch more than their allowed quota).

- Over time, new square segment netting would be introduced with larger size mesh for the protection of adolescent species.

- Fishing licenses would be allocated according to local needs to discourage larger industrial fishing vessels.

Fish stocks are already dangerously low due to over fishing but steps taken now to control the size of catches and to conserve stocks, could ensure that the British fishing industry has a sound future ahead of it.

Would you like to see these proposals to help the fishing industry introduced? Please tick one:

( ) Yes

( ) No

( ) I would like more information

National lottery

When the present lottery contract runs its term, we would like to set up the national lottery to become a non-profit making private company, with an independent board, and administration carefully regulated. We would also streamline the way that the charity money is allocated, restricting the total amount that can be spent on administration to a percentage of the money available. We would also like to see a national lottery website where the public can express their own views and vote as to how they would like the money spent.

Would you like to see these proposals for the National Lottery introduced? Please tick one:

( ) Yes

( ) No

( ) I would like more information

National sports academy

Some years ago there was much talk about a national sports academy being set up. The UK has, over the years, produced some excellent sportsmen and women but many sports are poorly funded and treated as amateur pursuits. Australia has had a sports academy for twenty years and has started to reap the benefits in recent international events. We would like to see the academy cover all sports and allow applications to be made as young as sixteen. At the moment youngsters who are interested in sport as a career are often encouraged to wait until they have left university, which, of course, is then too late!

Would you like to see these proposals for a national sports academy introduced? Please tick one:

> ( ) *Yes*
> ( ) *No*
> ( ) *I would like more information*

Football clubs and their members

We would also like to see some proposals adopted for football (soccer). Even though football is an important part of the UK's culture and is greatly enjoyed by much of the population, genuine supporters do not seem to get a good deal. We could for instance:

- review the structure of football administration by including representatives of football clubs' players and their supporters.

- streamline all the football governing bodies into one single organisation, with greater supporter representation (these representatives would be elected by the supporters).

- support the compulsive funding of supporters' organisations and sponsorship of local facilities.

- encourage football clubs to seek advice from supporters and their representatives on stewarding at games.

- introduce a more equitable system of revenue sharing between professional clubs at all levels.

- introduce safe, standing balconies if the supporters choose to introduce them.

- introduce laws to prohibit clubs selling their grounds without the prior consent of a majority vote of official supporters.

- introduce some type of shared ownership scheme whereby season ticket holders are given a specified percentage of shares and dividends in the value and profits of the club (after one year's membership of the club). These would include voting rights as shareholders.

- restrict ticket price increases to keep in line with the rate of inflation. Some of the lower priced tickets have increased by amounts well above the rate of inflation.

Would you like to see these proposals on football clubs introduced? Please tick one:

      ( ) *Yes*
      ( ) *No*
      ( ) *I would like more information*

Overseas development

The government now spends 1.2 per cent of the UK's gross national product supporting overseas development and environmental projects, but why isn't more of this money given directly to international British Charities to run projects on behalf of the British public? Charities such as Oxfam and Save the Children are much more efficient than government aid programmes. For instance in 2003 Save the Children only spent 10 per cent of the money they received on administration, 90 per cent of the money went to those who needed it.[25] It is estimated that with government projects 38 per cent of aid money is spent on administration.

Indeed some of the uses of public money for so-called overseas aid projects have been rather dubious, including projects such as the Malaysian Pergau Dam that illegally gave British aid in return for the sale of weapons. This project caused an enormous amount of environmental damage and the relocation of many indigenous people from their homes.[26] Charities might approach the government with projects that have been well researched such as a fresh-water project or a forest regeneration project and then the funds would be allocated in stages as the project progressed.

This would certainly mean more efficient use of aid money than the present system. It would also be possible to set up a government charity website to see where the money is being spent and to allow the public to suggest where it would like these funds to be spent.

Would you like to see these proposals on overseas aid introduced? Please tick one:

        ( ) Yes
        ( ) No
        ( ) I would like more information

BBC television

The BBC has a legacy of producing outstanding programmes but in recent years rather than aiming at creative excellence, we have witnessed the introduction of an internal market style management (at great cost) against a lack of nurturing of genuine talent. One BBC insider described its structure as 'endless meetings, guidelines, mission statements and flow charts, which had no clear vision.'[27] The BBC needs to work harder to justify the yearly expenditure of the £3,382 million it receives from licence payers.[28] *Most of all it needs to allow its writers and producers the time and space to develop their skills to produce quality programming.*

The BBC could be producing world-class programmes but it needs a charter and leadership that appreciates that 'excellence' is more than just useful management speak. The BBC remains one of the most well-respected broadcasting services in the world but its structure now leaves it vulnerable to government interference, which is affecting the quality and calibre of its programming.

We would propose that:

- the Head of BBC is elected by the licence payer rather than being appointed by the government.

- the BBC has a charter to have a specific remit of independence from civil servants.

- set out more clearly the BBC's responsibilities to the public.

- the board of governors would include elected representatives of the public.

- the BBC's income is guaranteed (adjusted against the rate of inflation) on the licence fee.

Would you like to see these proposals on the BBC introduced?

Please tick one:

( ) *Yes*

( ) *No*

( ) *I would like more information*

Europe

However, before many of the above measures can be taken, one further question would have to be asked. As this is a constitutional question, it would have to be put to all of the electorate (of Europe).

Would you prefer to withdraw from the European Union and instead negotiate trading agreements with its other European countries, similar to those which Norway and Switzerland?

Please tick one:

( ) *Yes*

( ) *No*

( ) *I would like more information*

Conclusion

Although some of these proposals may be controversial with direct democracy, we would have the right to vote against a proposal or raise an alternative proposal. Ultimately it would be the responsibility of the citizens of the host country to guide government policy not politicians. The above subjects only cover some of the areas that would be addressed.

Others areas for discussion include: the welfare system; judiciary; agriculture; food and produce (particularly small producers); business exporting; transport strategy; housing; house buying and many other subjects that you may have thoughts on. These are areas that have been titled under our discussion forum on the direct democracy international website at:

www.directdemocracyinternational.com

Chapter Twelve

Further Questions on Direct Democracy

At the beginning of this book, we outlined how direct democracy might work. In this chapter I would like to address some final questions about direct democracy.

Who would oversee a working model of direct democracy?
One of the most important positions within any system of direct democracy is the people's chancellor. The People's Chancellor would be someone politically neutral who was elected by the people. The office of the People's Chancellor would be independent of government with a charter that guaranteed no interference from central government. One of the prerequisites for candidates applying for the position would be that they had not belonged to a political party in the last ten years. All candidates would also have to have some professional experience of the judicial system.

Who would make decisions about what was to be proposed in any given referendum?
This would be contained within a written constitution that would clearly state which decisions were to be made by government and which decisions were to be made by the public. There are a limited amount of areas that would remain in the remit of the government and these would include defence, the intelligence services and national security. Although it would be possible for voters to make

a proposal of intent on all government policy, the People's Chancellor and his/her office would have a specific area over which they would have jurisdiction and this would be set out in a clearly in a legal document.

What would the questions look like?

In California where referendums are quite common, the proposer has to put the question/or questions into a substantive and legal document, with a summary question that the electorate can either support or not. Questions would, of course, have to be clear and concise.

Would it cost a lot of money to introduce direct democracy?

Initially, there would be costs involved but what Switzerland has found is that governments spend less when they have to be accountable for their spending.

Could anyone sign the petition?

We would envisage that everyone would have a voting number that would have to be quoted when signing the proposal and this could be contained on a secure identity card. Only citizens of each particular country would be able to sign petitions and there would be strict penalties for those involved in fraud.

Why are initiatives only accepted if over 50 per cent of the electorate vote?

This is only one option but it has the advantage that the proposal would have to gain overwhelming support from the electorate. It also stops groups of activists from forcing through legislation that the majority of people do not want. Although the '50 per cent plus one vote' hurdle seems a lot, with the introduction of new voting measures such as allowing voting over a period of a week, email voting, postal voting, telephone and internet voting, more people will be able and willing to vote. The '50 per cent plus one vote' rule would be set out within the written constitution but could be amended if enough people voted to do so.

There are other alternatives, such as:

- a quorum of not less than say 40 per cent (arbitrary figure) of eligible voters would be needed to support an initiative, or

- any majority is acceptable (no matter how many people voted).

- to make voting compulsory but provide a tick box for voters to state that they do not support any of the options available (the introduction of compulsory voting would have to be voted on by the electorate).

What if the government tried to overrule the people?
The written constitution would make it clear who holds power in which areas, as well as putting in place the appropriate checks and balances against abuses by the executive. Within a written constitution it would be stated that the people had the right to call a referendum on all subjects with named exceptions (such as defence or national security).

What if the proposer of an initiative changed their mind?
Anyone who proposed an initiative could withdraw the initiative in the 180 days that they have to collect the 2 per cent of signatures required. If enough support had been reached at the end of the 180 day period, the referendum would go ahead.

What if legislation goes through that you don't like?
At the present time, governments frequently make decisions that many people don't like, yet the electorate have no recourse to change

them. It would be for the People's Chancellor to look at all proposals and be the final arbiter of what could be put in a referendum. It is unlikely that any initiative would be acceptable to everybody but this is still fairer than decisions being made that the majority of people do not want!

Would we have bigoted or racist laws?
We would set clear and binding restrictions to protect minority groups over questions of gender, ethnicity or religion.

What about regional variation?
The People's Chancellor would be given the task of protecting the rights of smaller regional areas. Local and regional areas would be free to have local referendums on local issues.

Who decides whether it's a local issue?
We already have a system in place whereby local authorities have authority over specific local issues.

Wouldn't the media be able to unfairly influence decisions?
Campaigning on any issues would be halted two weeks before a referendum took place, similar to the elections now. We could also introduce a bill that would give people the right of reply in the press. France has a system whereby anyone who feels they have been unfairly slandered by the press can apply to a court to have a right of reply. The reply has to be printed in the newspaper or magazine within a set period of time and has to be no longer than five hundred words. The same would apply to television and radio, where the person would have the right to reply. Interestingly, in France it has had the effect of tempering the excesses of the media and has reduced the amount of libels cases that have come to court.

Would we not have large corporations campaigning on issues?
We would only allow private citizens to campaign on initiatives.
Anyone campaigning would have to register and declare any interests that they had. A similar rule applies in other countries that use
a system of direct democracy.

How do you put a limit on the cost of proposals?
Any proposal that is put forward would also have to state quite
clearly the anticipated cost. Not all referendum proposals would
be about spending money. Proposals that would save money could
also be raised. In Switzerland, research by Clive Church has shown
that government spending fell sharply when government was made
accountable to the taxpayer. As he says, 'direct democracy also con-
strains finance, more than is the case nationally.'[1] It would be set
out in the constitution, that each year government had to work
within a given budget without raising taxation further or borrow-
ing more money.

What about laws that already exist?
No laws would change unless the public voted to change them.
Any new legislation would supersede old legislation.

What if we have queries?
There will be many questions raised but none of these will be
insurmountable. We have the advantage of being able to look at the
Swiss, Norwegian, Danish and Californian systems that already use
different types of direct democracy.

Wouldn't politics be less exciting?
For the majority of people politics has become rather irrelevant.
With direct democracy the most exciting debates would involve
the general public who will ultimately decide on policy. The

majority of people are less interested in 'exciting' politics than having their public services run properly!

SUMMARY

Chapter Thirteen

Working Together

There is no doubt that the introduction of direct democracy faces an enormous challenge. It is up against well-funded and established political parties but direct democracy has one enormous advantage. It has the support of the public. For the first time ever we could be looking at the beginnings of a truly democratic movement that is not controlled by politicians but by the people. Years ago when I started researching this book there was nowhere near as much interest in the subject, now there are many people all working towards the same ends.

Democratic unaccountability is endemic in most democracies. *For all our criticisms of the UK, there are many countries where problems of lack of accountability are far worse.* In researching this book I did not have the time or resources to look at each and every country in detail but the need for direct democracy is widespread. The public no longer need to trust the whims and foibles of elected politicians to make decisions on their behalf.

Although many people around the world will no doubt have more questions about direct democracy, we only need look to the system that has been in place in Switzerland for over a hundred years to see that it is possible. Maybe at last there is an answer to the vision and identity each nation wants to adopt. Maybe at last people will be given the responsibility to make their own choices.

Direct Democracy International

Direct democracy International is a fully independent organisation that relies on the public for support and which actively campaigns for the introduction of direct democracy around the world. Direct Democracy International is a virtual centre, its main point of contact being the website. This keeps costs to a minimum but at the same time allows the message about direct democracy to reach as many people as possible around the world. If you would like more information about what we do, logon to:

www.directdemocracyinternational.com

The website contains useful links, bibliographies, campaign details and an international discussion forum. You can support Direct Democracy International by:

- emailing our website address to family, friends and colleagues: (see above).

- setting up a campaign group in your area.

- becoming involved in one of our many campaigns to raise support and awareness for direct democracy.

- visiting our online shop or by making a donation directly to Direct Democracy International.

- *most importantly - you can talk to other people about direct democracy* - to explain how we could all benefit from its introduction.

GLOSSARY

Act of Parliament: the formally codified result of Parliament making legislation.

Affidavit: declaration in writing made upon oath.

AGM: annual general meeting.

ATM: automated telling machine used for dispensing cash.

Baronet: (in Britain) a commoner who holds the lowest hereditary title.

Bill of Rights: an English statute of 1689 guaranteeing the rights and liberty of the individual subject.

Black Rod: an officer in the House of Lords whose main duty is summoning Parliament.

British Isles: a group of islands in Western Europe consisting of Great Britain, Ireland, the Isle of Man, Orkney, the Shetland Islands and the Channel Islands.

BSE: Bovine Spongiform Encephalopathy is a disease of cattle first identified in 1986 (sometimes known as 'mad cow' disease).

Bond market: a market in the guarantee of payments against an agreed loan.

CBI: Confederation of British Industry.

Cabinet minister: the executive and policy making body of government closest to the Prime Minister.

Cabinet office: senior department of government.

Census: official periodic count of a population.

Central Intelligence Agency: a federal US bureau that collects intelligence information.

Chancellor of the Exchequer: British cabinet minister responsible for finance.

Chief executive: senior executive within an organisation or company.

Chief Whip: senior business manager found in all parliamentary political parties.

CIA: Central Intelligence Agency.

City of London: Home to the financial and money markets of London.

Civil servant: a member of the civil service.

Civil service: a body responsible for the public administration of Britain and the British government.

Collective cabinet responsibility: (see page 53).

Common Market: Western European Economic association created by the Treaty of Rome in 1958. Later called the European Economic Community, and then the European Union.

Community Charge: local tax for residents within a regional area, based on property.

Commissioner: senior person who is authorised to make economic and political decisions on behalf of the European Union.

Conservative Party: politically right-of-centre party that developed from the Tories in the late 1830s in Britain.

Constituency: the body of voters who elect one representative.

Constitution: the fundamental political principles on which a state is governed.

Coronation: the act or ceremony of crowning a monarch.

County Chief Constable: (see page 185).

County Health Directors: (see page 176).

County Health Trust: (see page 177).

CPS: Crown Prosecution service.

(the) Crown: the sovereignty or realm of a monarch.

Customs and Excise: British government department with responsibility for collecting import and export duties, including VAT (value added tax).

DfES: Department for Education and Skills.

DG: Directorates-General (see page 155).

Downing Street: 10 Downing Street, the home of the British Prime Minister.

ECB: European Central Bank.

ECSC: European Coal and Steel Community.

EEC: European Economic Community.

Electorate: those people legally entitled to vote in any election.

Elizabeth II: Britain's constitutional monarch and Head of State.

EMU: European Monetary Union.

ERM: Exchange Rate Mechanism.

EU: the European Union.

EURATOM: European Atomic Energy Community.

Euro: principal currency of the European Union.

Europhobic: term often used in a derogatory sense of those who are sceptical about political union with Europe.

Executive: a body of Crown minsiters, responsible to the Prime Minister.

Federalism: a form of government where power is divided between one central and several regional government bodies.

GDP: gross domestic product.

General election: British election held at least every five years to elect the government of Britain.

General Practitioner: a doctor who does not specialise in one area of medicine but has a medical practice.

Green card: a document that entitles its holder to conditional residence within the US.

Green paper: a paper outlining a parliamentary proposal for the consultation of MPs.

GNP: gross national product.

GP: see General Practitioner.

Head of State: the most senior person in any political system. In the United Kingdom the Head of State is Queen Elizabeth II.

House of Lords: the senior chamber of the British Parliament composed of peers of the realm.

House of Representatives: in the United States, the lower Chamber of Congress; in Australia, the lower Chamber of Parliament.

IMF: International Monetary Fund.

Income tax: progressive personal tax levied on income.

Initiative: a device to introduce legislation within a democratic body.

Inland Revenue: British government body responsible for collecting personal and corporate tax.

Investiture: the act of presenting a title or the insignia of office.

ISB: Individual Schools Budget (see page 181).

Lord Chancellor: cabinet minister who is head of the judiciary in England and Wales and Speaker of the House of Lords.

Jacobite: an adherent of James II after he was overthrown in 1688, or followers of his descendants seeking to regain the throne.

Judiciary: the central branch of the state concerned with the administration of justice.

King's Counsel: a barrister appointed Counsel to the Crown on the recommendation of the Lord Chancellor, entitled to sit within the bar of the court and to wear a silk gown (used when the monarch is male).

Labour Party: British political party formed around 1900, an amalgam of various trade union bodies and socialist groups.

LEA: local education authority.

LSC: Learning and Skills Council.

Legislature: parliamentary body vested with the power to make, amend and repeal law.

Liberal Party: British political party, successor to the Whigs, which was a dominant political force in the nineteenth century.

Macro economic: branch of economics concerned with aggregates such as national income, consumption and investment.

Magna Carta: the charter granted by King John at Runnymede in 1215, recognising the rights and privileges of the barons, church and freeman.

Manifesto: a public declaration of intent and policies.

MEP: European Member of Parliament.

Minister: a person appointed to head a government department.

MP: (British) Member of Parliament, who is a member of the House of Commons at Westminster.

NATO: North Atlantic Treaty Organisation.

NAO: National Audit Office.

NCC: National Curriculum Council.

NDPB: non-departmental public body.

New Labour: the new name of the Labour Party since the late 1990s.

NHS: National Health Service.

No '10': 10 Downing Street, the home of the British Prime Minister.

Nolle prosequi: an entry made on the court record, when a plaintiff in a civil suit or prosecutor in a criminal prosecution, undertakes not to continue the action of prosecution.

OBE: Order of the British Empire, an honour awarded in Britain for services to the country.

OFSTED: Office for Standards in Education.

OLAF: European Anti-Fraud Office.

Opinion poll: canvassing of a representative group in order to determine a general opinion on a subject.

Palace of Westminster: centre of British government including all main and surrounding buildings within the Westminster complex.

Parliament: the highest legislative authority in Britain, consisting of the House of Commons, the House of Lords and the sovereign.

PCS: Parliamentary Commissioner on Standards.

Parliamentary Initiative: (see page 18).

Peer: a person who holds any of the five grades of British nobility including Duke, marquess, earl, viscount and baron with entitlement to sit in the House of Lords.

Personnel Recall Initiatives: (see page 19).

Petitioning: a formal request usually in writing to a government authority.

Petition of Rights: a formal request containing proposed rights for individuals.

People's Chancellor: (see page 25).

PIN: personal identification number often used in conjunction with bank cards.

Prime Minister: the head of a parliamentary government.

Privy councillor: a member of the private council of the British sovereign.

Proposal: a document containing a proposed piece of legislation or a change in the law.

Proposer: A person who has initiated a proposal.

Polling station: a centre used for the recording of voters' choices, often a government building.

Popular initiative: (see page 17).

PAU: Public Appointments Unit.

Prerogative: a power privilege or immunity restricted to a sovereign or sovereign government.

Presbyterian: relating to any of various Protestant churches governed by presbyters or lay elders usually adhering to modified forms of Calvinism.

Prince Regent: George IV as regent of Great Britain and Ireland during the insanity of his father.

QCA: Qualifications and Curriculum Authority.

Quango: quasi-autonomous national government organisation, independent in theory from the department that created it, nominally under the control of the minister who appoints its members and sets its budget.

Queen's Counsel: a barrister appointed Counsel to the Crown on the recommendation of the Lord Chancellor, entitled to sit within the bar of the court and to wear a silk gown.

Quorum: a minimum number of voters in an election required to be present before any initiative can be accepted.

Republic: a form of government where the people or the elected representatives possess the supreme power.

Second chamber: Parliamentary House of Lords.

Select committee: Cross bench committee that discusses and advises on government legislation.

Senate: the upper chamber of the legislatures of the US, Canada, Australia and other democracies.

Short money: (see page 76).

Single issue party: a political party formed to campaign for one issue.

Sovereignty: a person exercising supreme power such as a monarch.

Spin: political term used to emphasise the positive aspects of a situation or government policy.

Statute law: a law enacted by a legislative body.

Subsidiarity: (see page 139).

Suffragette: a female advocate of the extension of franchise (the right to vote for government) for women as seen at the beginning of the twentieth century in Britain.

'talked out': a parliamentary device used to halt the progression of a parliamentary bill by talking past the allocated time allowed.

TAO: technical assistance office.

TTA: Teacher Training Agency.

WTO: World Trade Organisation.

Tory: a member of the Conservative Party.

Treasury: the government department in charge of finance and economic strategy.

Treaty of the European Union: (see page 139).

TTA: Teacher Training Agency.

Referendum: submission of an issue of public importance to the direct vote of the electorate.

UN: United Nations.

United Kingdom: Great Britain and Northern Ireland.

VAT: value added tax.

Visa: an endorsement, usually in a passport, signifying that the bearer has the right to travel through the issuing country.

Whig: a conservative member of the Liberal Party.

Whips office: the office of the Whips, the Parliamentary managers responsible for maintaining party political discipline.

FOOTNOTES

Introduction

1 United Kingdom National Office of Statistics.
2 Ibid.
3 Carswell D. Direct Democracy: Empowering People to Make Their Lives Better. Cchange; 2002.
4 news.bbc.co.uk/1/hi/uk_politics/196665569
5 'Guiding Principles: Public Attitudes towards Conflict in Public Life' National Centre for Social Research into Elections and Social Trends, January 2003.
6 news.bbc.co.uk/1/hi/uk_politics/196665569 and Published Expenditure Statistical Analyses 2003 - corrigendum corrected tables for Chapter 8.
7 United Kingdom National Office of Statistics.
8 www.parliament.uk Official House of Commons website
9 Moore M. Stupid White Men. Penguin; 2001.
10 Barnett A. This Time: Our Constitutional Revolution. Vintage; 1997.

Chapter 1 - What is Direct Democracy?

1 www.telegraph.co.uk/money/main Feb 2003.
2 money telegraph.co.uk/money/main March 2003.
3 www.money telegraph.co.uk/money/main Feb 2004.
4 www.telegraph.co.uk/money/main Feb 2003.
5 money telegraph.co.uk/money/main Dec 2002.
6 www.guardian.co.uk/lords/story Feb 2003.
7 www.parliament.uk Official House of Commons website.
8 www.economist .co.uk/countries Britain/profile Feb 2003.
9 Thatcher M. The Downing Street Years. London: HarperCollins; 1993.
10 Seaton N. The True Cost of State Education. Centre for Policy Studies; 2002.
11 Ibid.
12 www.hm-treasury.gov.uk European Union Finance
13 www.personneltoday.com/Article16632.htm
14 The Electoral Commission - www.parliament.uk/commons/lib/research
15 www.iht.com/articles/128654
16 http://news.bbc.co.uk - BBC News website February 2004
17 Switzerland's New Federal Constitution. Translated by Karrer P. 1998. Section 4: People and Cantons, Article 138 and Article 139.
18 Wallace-Macpherson M. Citizens Initiative and Referendum - Prospects for More Democracy in Great Britain.
19 www.swissinfo.org/sen/Swissinfo Jan 2004
20 Table K202 Age Structure Local Authorities and Boroughs Census 2000/1 and www.londonelects.org.uk/mayor/results/graphic1.html 2000 London Mayoral Election results.
21 Telegraph 10March 2004.
22 www.parliament.uk Official House of Commons website

23 Sigg O. Political Switzerland. Arts Council of Switzerland, CH-8024 Zurich.

24 www.railway-technology.com/projects/switzerland Feb 2003

25 Initiative and Referendum Institute at the University of Southern California Report 2003

26 US Census Bureau, Statistical Abstract of the United States 2003.

27 Baston L. Sleaze - The State of Britain. Macmillan for Channel 4 Television; 2000.

28 Ibid.

29 Written answer from the House of Commons information service www.parliament.uk/faq/lords 2003.

30 State of the Nation 1995. Research conducted on behalf of Joseph Rowntree Trust Limited. May 1995

31 Jos Verhulst www.ping.be/jvwi t/directdemocracynow.html

Chapter 2 - A Beautiful Democracy

1   Jones N. The Control Freaks. Politico's; 2002.

2   Ibid.

3   Ibid.

4   Barnett H. Britain Unwrapped. Penguin Books; 2002.

5   Jones N. The Control Freaks. Politico's; 2002.

6   Ibid.

7   Marr A. Ruling Britannia. Michael Joseph; 1995.

8   Jones N. The Control Freaks. Politico's; 2002.

9   www.bbcnews.co.uk/1/hi Sept 2000

10 www.parliament.uk Official House of Commons website.

11 Baston L. Sleaze - The State of Britain. Macmillan for Channel 4 Television; 2000.

12 Conduct Unbecoming. Eds Gay O. & Leopold P. Politico's; 2004.

13 Ibid.

14 Dixon P. The Truth about Westminster. Kingsway Publications; 1996.

15 Conduct Unbecoming. Eds Gay O.& Leopold P. Politico's; 2004.

16 Ibid.

17 Ibid.

18 Hansard Debate 13 February 2002.

19 Dixon P. The Truth about Westminster. Kingsway Publications; 1996.

20 Ibid.

21 Gorman T. The Bastards: Dirty Tricks and the Challenge to Europe. Pan Books; 1993.

22 Ibid.

23 www.parliament.uk Official House of Commons website.

24 Gorman T. The Bastards: Dirty Tricks and the Challenge to Europe. Pan Books; 1993.

25 de Smith S.A Constitutional and Administrative Law. Penguin; 1971.

26 Mackintosh J. The British Cabinet, 3rd Ed. Stevens; 1977.

27 Dixon P. The Truth about Westminster. Kingsway Publications; 1996.

28 Register of MPs' Interests 1995. Hansard (ref:186 1994-1995).

29 Manucuso M. The Ethical World of British MPs. McGill-Queens University Press; 1995.

30 John S. The Persuaders. Palgrave Macmillan; 2002.

31 Ibid.

32 Hansard 110 Session 1986-87.

33 The American Way of Influence - Observer 19 July 1998, citing Larry Matkinson from the Centre for Responsive Politics in Washington.

34 Citing Steve John, The Persuaders - researching the Public Policy Unit organisation.

35 John S. The Persuaders. Palgrave Macmillan; 2002.

36 'Cash for Questions' article by S.Bates, Guardian 11 July 1994.

37 The Times 8 July 1997.

38 'Lobbying's High Priest Admitted Paying MPs' article in The Times, 21 October 1994

39 Barnett A. This Time: Our Constitutional Revolution. Vintage; 1997.

40 'Regularise the Regulator: MPs Should Let Mrs Filkin Stay at her Job,' Guardian 16 November 2001.

41 Baston L. Sleaze - The State of Britain. Macmillan for Channel 4 Television; 2000.

42 Dixon P. The Truth about Westminster. Kingsway Publications; 1996.

43 Democratic Audit of Britain - Charter 88 from the University of Essex 1994.

44 Ibid.

45 Marr A. Ruling Britannia. Michael Joseph; 1995.

46 Article by Jerome Burne on vitamin supplements, Independent 23 July 1997.

47 Marr A. Ruling Britannia. Michael Joseph; 1995.

48 Ibid.

49 Barnett A. This Time: Our Constitutional Revolution. Vintage; 1997.

50 Challen C. Price of Power. Vision Paperbacks; 1998.

51 Daily Telegraph, 21 December 1994.

52 Countryside Commission News, March 1991.

53 Marr A. Ruling Britannia. Michael Joseph; 1995.

54 Ibid.

55 Barnett A. This Time: Our Constitutional Revolution. Vintage; 1997.

56 Stuart Weir the Democratic Audit, cited in Ruling Britannia by Andrew Marr. Michael Joseph; 1995.

57 Marr A. Ruling Britannia. Michael Joseph; 1995.

58 Ibid.

59 Barnett A. This Time: Our Constitutional Revolution. Vintage; 1997.

60 Monbiot G. Captive State -The Corporate Takeover of Britain. Pan Books.

61 Ibid.

62 Ibid.

63 Ibid.

64 Ibid.

65 Ibid.

66 Ibid.

67 Field J. The Story of Parliament. Politico's Publishing; 2002.

Chapter 3 - Pulling the Strings of Power

1   Challen C. Price of Power. Vision Paperbacks; 1998.

2   Baston L. Sleaze - The State of Britain. Macmillan for Channel 4 Television 2000.

3   The Times 29 May 2003.

4   Ewing K.D. Trade Unions, the Labour Party and Political Funding. Catalyst; 2002.

5   www.electoralcommission.org.uk.uk/media-centre

6   Daily Express 24 February 1995.

7   Ibid.

8   Dixon P. The Truth about Westminster. Kingsway Publications; 1996.

9   Independent 15 May 1995.

10 Sunday Times 14 April 2002.

11 Guardian 13 April 2002.

12 Guardian 13 April 2002 and Scotland on Sunday 14 April 2002.

13 Independent 13 May 2002.

14 The Times 15 April 2002.

15 Jones N. The Control Freaks. Politico's; 2002.

16 Guardian15 April 2002.

17 N. Baker MP, Hansard Debate, 22 January 2001.

18 Ewing K.D. Trade Unions, the Labour Party and Political Funding. Catalyst; 2002.

19 www.acountancyage.com/New Feb 2004

20 Cole G.D.H. A History of the Labour Party Since 1914. 1948.

21 Ewing K.D. Trade Unions, the Labour Party and Political Funding. Catalyst; 2002.

22 Jones B. Politics. Pearson Longman; 1991.

23 Dixon P. The Truth about Westminster. Interview between Lord Healey and Dr Patrick Dixon, 17 May 1995. Kingsway Publications; 1996.

24 Dixon P. The Truth about Westminster, 1974-5 Yorkshire Area Council of the National Union. Kingsway Publications; 1996.

25 Clause 2 Labour Party Constitutional Rules.

26 Ewing K.D. Trade Unions, the Labour Party and Political Funding. Catalyst; 2002.

27 Challen C. Price of Power. Vision Paperbacks; 1998.

28 Ibid.

29 Barnett A. This Time: Our Constitutional Revolution. Vintage; 1997.

30 Challen C. Price of Power. Vision Paperbacks; 1998.

31 Ibid.

32 Ibid.

33 Ibid.

34 Ibid.

35 Sunday Times 19 May 1996.

36 Challen C. Price of Power. Vision Paperbacks; 1998.

37 Sunday Times 27 July 1997.

38 Guardian 19 September 1991.

39 Challen C. Price of Power. Vision Paperbacks; 1998.

40 Guardian 4 September 1996.

41 Report from the National Audit Office.

42 Observer 15 September 1996.

43 Challen C. Price of Power. Vision Paperbacks; 1998.

44 Ibid.

45 Barnett A. This Time: Our Constitutional Revolution. Vintage; 1997.

FOOTNOTES

46 Independent on Sunday 16 October 1994.
47 Challen C. Price of Power. Vision Paperbacks; 1998.
48 Ibid.
49 Guardian 16 February 1998.
50 Barnett H. Britain Unwrapped. Penguin Books; 2002.
51 Ibid.
52 Ewing K.D. Trade Unions, the Labour Party and Political Funding. Catalyst; 2002.

Chapter 4 - Monarchy and Parliament

1 Field J. The Story of Parliament. Politico's Publishing; 2002.
2 Gorman T. The Bastards: DirtyTricks and the Challenge to Europe. Pan Books; 1993.
3 Field J. The Story of Parliament. Politico's Publishing; 2002.

Chapter 5 - The Missing Constitution

1 Guardian 28 April 1997, report on the Child Poverty Action group.
2 Barnett A. This Time: Our Constitutional Revolution. Vintage; 1997.
3 Amery L.S. Thoughts on the Constitution. Oxford University Press; 1964.
4 Barnett A. This Time: Our Constitutional Revolution. Vintage; 1997.
5 Norton P. The Constitution in Flux. Oxford: Martin Robertson; 1982.
6 Dicey A.V. Introduction to the Study of the Law of the Constitution. Macmillan; 1885.
7 The Scottish Claim of Right 1988.
8 Tony Blair - Cardiff speech 1994.
9 The Constitution of Britain. Institute for Public Policy Research; 1991.
10 Jenkins S. Accountable to None: The Tory Nationalization of Britain. London; 1995.
11 Carr E.H. What is History? Macmillan; 1961.

Chapter 7 - Elizabeth II

1 Bradford S. Elizabeth. New York: Farrar, Straus and Giroux; 1996.
2 Written reply from Buckingham Palace.
3 Elizabeth II on BBC television.
4 Bagehot W. The English Constitution, 1867. Republished by Fontana; 1993.
5 Daily Mail - 1 June 1997.
6 www.geography.about.com/library/weekly Feb 2003.
7 National Audit Office Report 2004.

Chapter 8 - The European Union

1 Bradford De Long J. The Economic History of the Twentieth Century. University of California at Berkeley and NBER Fen; 1997.
2 Winston Churchill's speech September 1946 Zurich conference.
3 Anderson P. Under the Sign of the Interim. London Review of Books 4 January 1994.
4 Maclay M. The European Union. Sutton; 1998.
5 Ibid.
6 Heath E. The Course of My Life. Hodder & Stoughton; 1998.

7 Edward Heath's speech to the Council of the WEU, 1962.
8 Edward Heath lecture at Harvard University USA 1967.
9 Barnett H. Britain Unwrapped. Penguin Books; 2002.
10 Connolly B. The Rotten Heart of Europe. Faber & Faber; 1995.
11 Otmar Issing http://news.bbc.co.uk/1/hi/business

Chapter 9 - What Difference Does It Make?

1 Barnett A. This Time: Our Constitutional Revolution, poll conducted in the Daily Telegraph. Vintage; 1997.
2 National Audit Office - Annual Report of the European Court of Auditors for the year 2000. Report by the Comptroller and Auditor General HC 859 Session 2001-2002: 30 May 2002.
3 New Report Financial Management in the European Union. The European Court of Auditors Report for the year 2001. HC 701 Session 2002-2003: 12 June 2003. HC 701 Session 2002-2003: 12 June 2003.
4 Van Buitenen P. Blowing the Whistle. Politico's; 2000.
5 Jean Monnet's United States of Europe Action Committee 1958.
6 Jenkins L. The Last Days of Britain. Orange State Press; 2001.
7 Ibid.
8 Ibid.
9 Silber L. & Little A. The Death of Yugoslavia. Penguin; 1996.
10 Jenkins L. The Last Days of Britain. Orange State Press; 2001.
11 National Audit Office - Annual Report of the European Court of Auditors for the year 2000. Report by the Comptroller and Auditor General HC 859 Session 2001-2002: 30 May 2002.
12 www.cec.org/info/embassy.htm
13 National Audit Office - Annual Report of the European Court of Auditors for the year 2000. Report by the Comptroller and Auditor General HC 859 Session 2001-2002: 30 May 2002.
14 www.bbc.co.uk/1/hi/uk_politics 28 October 1999.
15 Barnett A. This Time: Our Constitutional Revolution. Vintage; 1997.
16 Daily Mail Glance Back Books. Chepstow, 6 May 2001.
17 Jenkins L. The Last Days of Britain. Orange State Press; 2001.
18 Bank of England Working Paper no 102. Bridget and Nolan.
19 www.euro.co.uk/ general/bulletin 180
20 Living in Italy magazine, 'Euro Money or Your Life', Fiona Tankard.
21 Adair Turner, CBI Director General, quoted in Freedom Today Aug/Sept 1998.
22 www.news.bbc. co.uk/1/hi/world/europe/947798
23 www.eubusiness.com/afp 1/3/04
24 Directive number 1677/88 of 15 June 1988.
25 Jenkins L. The Last Days of Britain. Orange State Press; 2001.

Chapter 10 - The EU and the Missing Millions

1 National Audit Office - Annual Report of the European Court of Auditors for the year 2000. Report by the Comptroller and Auditor General HC 859 Session 2001-

FOOTNOTES

2002: 30 May 2002; and Financial Management in the European Union. The European Court of Auditors Report for the year 2001. HC 701 Session 2002-2003: 12 June 2003 HC 701 Session 2002-2003: 12 June 2003.

2   Van Buitenen P. Blowing the Whistle. Politico's; 2000.

3   National Audit Office - Annual Report of the European Court of Auditors for the year 2000. Report by the Comptroller and Auditor General HC 859 Session 2001-2002: 30 May 2002.

4   Ibid.

5   Ibid.

6   Ibid.

7   Ibid.

8   Ibid.

9   Van Buitenen P. Blowing the Whistle. Politico's 2000.

10 Ibid.

11 National Audit Office - Annual Report of the European Court of Auditors for the year 2000. Report by the Comptroller and Auditor General HC 859 Session 2001-2002: 30 May 2002.

12 Van Buitenen P. Blowing the Whistle. Politico's 2000.

13 National Audit Office - Annual Report of the European Court of Auditors for the year 2000. Report by the Comptroller and Auditor General HC 859 Session 2001-2002: 30 May 2002.

14 Van Buitenen P. Blowing the Whistle. Politico's 2000.

15 Ibid.

16 Panorama BBC Television 9 June 1999.

17 National Audit Office - Annual Report of the European Court of Auditors for the year 2000. Report by the Comptroller and Auditor General HC 859 Session 2001-2002: 30 May 2002.

18 Daily Telegraph November 2003.

19 National Audit Office - Annual Report of the European Court of Auditors for the year 2000. Report by the Comptroller and Auditor General HC 859 Session 2001-2002: 30 May 2002.

20 Gorman T. The Bastards: Dirty Tricks and the Challenge to Europe. Pan Books; 1993.

21 Financial Management in the European Union. The European Court of Auditors Report for the year 2001. HC 701 Session 2002-2003 12 June 2003, HC 701 Session 2002-2003 12 June 2003.

22 European Journal. 'Brusselsbourger' Matthew Elliot.

23 Ibid.

24 The Times 6 March 2004.

25 Daily Telegraph February 2002.

26 Daily Telegraph November 2003.

Chapter 11 - Direct Democracy Discussion Forum

1   The Times 6 March 2004.

2   House of Commons debate, Criteria for Appraisals by the National Institute for Clinical Excellence. Mr John Denham Hansard. 15 June 1999.

3   BBC News 24.

4   Redwood J. 'Power to Parents.' Centre for Policy Studies; 2002.

5   Seaton N. The True Cost of State Education. Centre for Policy Studies; 2002.

6   Ibid.

7   Ibid.

8   Ibid.

9   Ibid.

10 Boles N. The Centre Cannot Hold. Politico's: 2001.

11 Daily Telegraph April 2002.

12 www.manchesteronline.co.uk/news/stories/detail

13 Carswell D. Direct Democracy: Empowering People to Make Their Lives Better. Cchange; 2002.

14 Kirtzman A. Rudy Giuliani - Emperor of the City. Perennial; 2001.

15 Ibid.

16 Ibid.

17   Jones B. Politics. Pearson Longman; 1991.

18 Case of Adan and Aitseguer, Lords' Ruling 19 December 2000.

19 Home Office immigration figures June 2000.

20 Ibid.

21 www.bbc.co.uk/news/2/hi_news politics 8 March 2004.

22 Marr A. Ruling Britannia. Michael Joseph; 1995.

23 www.nesta.org.uk

24 'Causes, Concerns and Cures' quoted by Trevor Smith. Ridley & Doig.

25 Dawn Dunn - Save the Children Fiscal Accounts 2003.

26 Barnett A. This Time: Our Constitutional Revolution. Vintage; 1997.

27 Curran J. & Seaton J. Power Without Responsibility: the Press and Broadcasting in Britain. Routledge; 1985.

28 BBC Annual Report and Accounts 2001/2002.

Chapter 12 - Further Questions on Direct Democracy

1   Church C.H. The Politics and Government of Switzerland. Palgrave Macmillan; 2002.

INDEX

Acambis of Cambridge - 68
Adam Smith Institute - 62
advertising - 27
Advisory Committee on Novel Foods - 59
affidavit - 18
agriculture - 83
Al Gore - 9
Alastair Campbell - 44, 98
Albert Venn Dicey - 97
Albright and Wilson - 63
alcohol advertising - 15
Alex Salmond - 50
Andrew Kirtzman - 187
Andrew Marr - 46
Andrew Mitchell - 50
Angles - 105
Anglo-Saxons - 105
Anthony Barker - 58
Anthony Barnett - 56, 96
Anthony Eden - 86, 117
Argentina - 88
Aristide Briand - 130
Arnold Schwarzenegger - 19
arteriosclerosis - 116
Asil Nadir - 71
Asylum and Immigration Act - 189
asylum applicants - 189
ATMs - 21
Australia - 7, 200
Austria - 27, 85
Azerbaijan Republic (the) - 55
Bagehot - 117
Bahamas (The) - 115
Bank of Credit and Commerce - 72
Bank of England - 151
Barbara Castle - 48
Baroness Denton - 61
baronets - 83
Barry Sheerman - 75

Battle - 105
Battle of Culloden - 110
Battle of Hastings - 105
Battle of Naseby - 81
Battle of the Boyne - 110
Battle of Waterloo - 111
BBC - 46, 98, 139, 203
Belfry Hotel - 175
Belgium - 33, 134
Belize - 75
Benelux countries - 134
Berlin Airlift - 116
Berlin Wall - 88
Bernard Connolly - 138
Bernie Ecclestone - 68
Betty Boothroyd - 65
Bill of Rights Act - 94, 109
Birmingham - 82
'Blowing the Whistle' - 154
Bonnie Prince Charlie - 110
Bosnia - 73
Botnar - 72
Bourbons (the) - 130
Bristol - 17
Britain - 133, 147
British Airways - 56, 63
British aristocracy - 82
British Rail - 60
British Virgin Islands - 55
Brussels - 29, 133
Bruton Street - 113
BSE (mad cow disease) - 150
Buckingham Palace - 53, 119
Bundesbank - 138
Business Age magazine - 72
by-elections - 20
Cadbury Schweppes - 56
California - 6, 15, 16, 19, 28, 30, 207
Callaghan - 87

INDEX

Cambridge - 81
Canadian - 113
Captain Ivanov - 87
Captive State - 63
career politicians - 10, 43
Carlisle - 110
Carnaby Street - 87
Cash for Questions - 55
Catholic Pope Adrian IV - 107
Catholicism - 107
CBI - 151
Celts - 105
Chairman of BP - 63
Chairman of Members'
 Interests Committee - 50
Churchill - (see Winston Churchill)
Chamberlain - 114
Chancellor of the Exchequer - 12, 84
Charles (Prince) - 80,81
Charles I - 79, 97, 108, 109
Charles II - 81, 109
Charter 88 campaign - 100
Chemical Industries Association - 63
Chief of Staff - 98
Chief Press Secretary - 98
Chief Whip - 47, 52
child abuse - 6
Chilean Reconciliation Movement - 55
China - 116
Chris Godsmark - 60
Chris Heaton - 162
Christian Wolmar - 60
Christianity - 104
Christine Keeler - 87
citizenship - 191
City of Hull - 198
City of London - 151
civil servants - 13, 44, 88, 94
class system - 106
Cleaner Vehicles Task Force - 64
Clive Church - 210
Code of Conduct and Ethics - 46, 56
Cold War - 86, 87, 89, 116

Colin Challen's - 71
collective cabinet responsibility - 53, 54
Colonel Abdel Nasser - 86
Comissioner Liikanen - 159
Commissioner Gradin - 159
Commissioner Van den Broek - 159
Common Campaigns Ltd - 67
Common Market (see EU)
Common's Public Gallery - 84
Commons Public Accounts Committee - 60
Commonwealth - 85, 117
Communists - 133
community charge - 13, 17, 19, 29, 193
Conference - 70
Conservative Party - 43, 52, 57, 66, 67, 72-74,
76, 83, 89, 136
Conservative Party Team 1000 - 75
constitutional monarch - 32
Corn Laws - 89
Cornwall - 17
Corruption Bill - 50
Council of Ministers - 132, 145
Countryside Agency - 63
County Armagh - 150
County Chief Constables - 185
County Landowners Association - 63
Court of Auditors - 157
CPS - 185
Cromwell (Oliver) 80-81, 108
Crown Prerogative - 97
Crown Prosecution Service - 185
Croydon - 17
Customs and Excise - 174
David Stewart - 45
David Tredinnick - 55
David Willett's - 50
Delours - 137
Democratic Audit of Britain - 59
Denmark - 15, 6, 28, 105, 114, 152
Department for Education and Skills - 14, 181
Department of Health - 174
Department of Trade and Industry - 63
Department of Transport - 60

232

INDEX

Derby - 110
Descartes - 109
Deutschmark - 138, 140
Devon - 17
DfES - 14, 181, 183
Dianne Abbott - 46
Direct Democracy International - 33, 34, 216
Director of Research Nestlé - 64
Directorates-General - 155
Dissolution of Parliament - 118
dividend tax credit - 12
Donald Dewar - 45
Doomsday Book - 105
Dorset - 17
Douglas Carswell's - 176
Downing Street - 7, 53, 87
Dr David Kelly - 45
Dr Johnson - 82
Dr Richard Taylor - 179
Duke of Wellington - 111
Duke of Windsor - 113, 115
Duncan Sandys - 134
Dunkirk - 114
e-voting - 21
E. H. Carr - 102
East Finchley - 88
Eastern Europe - 130
ECHO - 159
ECSC - 132
Edinburgh - 16, 110, 188
Edward Heath - 86, 87, 134-136
Edward I - 106
Edward III - 107
Edward VI - 107
Edward VIII - 113, 114
EEC - 133, 137
EGO - 60
Electra Fleming - 73
Electra Investment Trust plc - 74
electronic voting - 21
Elizabeth Filkin - 46, 56
Elizabeth I - 107
Elizabeth II - 99, 101, 113, 115, 120

Elizabeth's (II) coronation - 116
Elysée Palace - 135
Emma Nicholson - 74
England - 16, 80, 81, 83, 104, 110
English prayer book - 109
Enron - 69
Essex - 16
ethnic groups - 27
EU (European Union) - 14, 56, 87, 88, 95, 97, 130, 134-137, 140, 141, 143, 144, 149, 160, 190, 204
EU anti-fraud investigators - 162
EURATOM - 133
Euro currency - 15, 140, 141
Eurojust - 147
European Atomic Energy Community - 133
European Central Bank - 138, 141
European Coal and Steel Community - 132
European Commission - 160
European Court of Human Rights - 150
European Defence Community - 132
European Economic Community (also see EU) - 133, 134, 137
European Elections - 14, 144
European Federal State - 137
European High Court - 132
European Market - 133
European Monetary Union (EMU) - 138, 151
European Parliament - 47, 145
European Public Prosecutor - 148
European Union (see EU)
Eurostat - 161, 162
Ewen Cameron - 63
Exchange Rate Mechanism - 138, 140
Executive (the) - 100
Executive Commissariat - 132
Expeditionary forces - 114
expense abuses - 43
expenses - 47
extra government bodies - 13
Factorame - 150
Falkland Islands - 88
Fidel Castro - 86
Fiona Tankard - 151

First Minister of Scotland - 49
First World War - 17, 57, 84, 85, 114
fishing rights - 99
Ford UK - 64
Formula One - 68
France - 7, 27, 33, 82, 109, 111, 114, 133, 189
Francis Place - 111
French - 86, 111, 131
French National Assembly - 133
French revolution - 111
G Plan - 133
Gabriel Stauner - 162
Général Charles de Gaulle - 133
general election - 7, 9
General Medical Council - 118
General Pinochet - 55
genetically modified crops - 17, 23
George II - 110
George III - 111
George IV - 111
George Monbiot - 63
George V - 112
George VI - 113
George. W. Bush - 9
Germany - 33, 114, 131, 133, 134, 189
gilded political career paths - 31
Giovanni Di Stefano - 73
Glarus - 16
Global Climate Coalition - 64
GNP - 29, 148
Goering's - 115
Goldman Sachs - 151
Gordon Brown - 12, 47, 63, 67, 100
Government Prerogative - 97
Graham Riddick - 55
granting of honours - 98
Gray Davis - 19
Green Cards - 191
Gross Domestic Product (GDP) - 136
Gross National Product (GNP) - 8
Guernsey - 104
Gulf Wars - 116
Hambros - 73

Hampshire - 105
Hapsburgs (the) - 130
Harald Hardrada - 105
Harold Macmillan - 117, 133
Harold Wilson - 53, 87, 136
Harry S. Truman - 131
Hartlepool - 7, 8
Head of State - 32, 99
Heath (see Edward Heath)
Heathrow - 118
Helmut Kohl - 138
Henry Campbell-Bannerman - 89
Henry II - 105, 107
Henry McLeish - 49
Henry VII - 107
Henry VIII - 107
Her Majesty's Stationery Office - 73
Her Majesty's Treasury - 174
hereditary peers - 33
Hinduja brothers - 69
Hitler - 85
Holland - 68, 111, 115
Hong Kong - 87, 116
honours - 53
Horserace Totalisator Board - 61
Hotel Cecil - 83
House of Commons - 9, 18, 45, 48, 50, 51, 65, 85, 97, 98, 107
House of Commons Fees Office - 49
House of Congress - 25
House of Lords - 25, 33, 51, 97, 106, 112
House of Representatives - 9
Housing Corporation - 59
Howard Jarvis - 30
human rights - 99
Hutton inquiry - 45
Ian Greer's - 56
Ian McAllister - 64
immigration policy - 99
Incidental expenses - 47
Independent Labour Party - 83
Indian Family Pension Funds Body of Commissioners - 59

Industrial Research Trust - 67
initiative - 15
Inland Revenue - 50, 72, 73, 174
Innovation Courses - 197
Institute for Public Policy Research - 102
Institute of Directors - 146
Institute of Food Research - 64
intelligence services - 100
international law - 99
International Monetary Fund (IMF) - 95
IRA - 150
Iran-Iraq conflict - 72
Ireland - 109
Irish Parliament - 107
Isle of Man - 104
Italians - 16, 114, 134
Jack Cunningham - 63
Jacobean plot - 109
Jacques Delors - 137, 157
Jacques Santer - 160
James Callaghan - 53
James I - 108
James II - 109, 110
James VI - 108
Japan - 7, 87, 114, 137
Jean Monnet - 130, 131, 145
Jean-Jacques Rousseau - 7
Jeremy Bentham - 82
Jersey - 71, 104
John Beckworth - 75
John Kennedy - 73
John Latsis - 73
John Major - 43, 44, 98, 140
John Poulson - 88
John Prescott - 69
John Prideaux - 60
John Profumo - 86
Johnson - 108
Jonathan Powell - 44, 98
Joseph Rowntree Trust - 33
judiciary (the) - 100
Jutes (the) - 105
Karadzic - 73

Keir Hardie - 83
Keith Vaz - 50
Ken Livingstone - 22
Kent - 17
King Alfred - 105
King Edward VII - 112
King Edward VIII - 112, 113
King Harold - 105
King James I - 79
King William - 109
knighthoods - 57
Korean War - 116
L. S. Amery - 96
Labour Party (see New Labour) - 70, 89
Lakshmi Mittal - 68
Lancashire - 190
Learning and Skills Council - 181
LEAs - 14, 181, 184
Leeds - 82
Leonardo da Vinci programme - 158
Liberal Party - 57, 74, 76, 83, 85, 89
Liechtenstein - 72
Lincolnshire - 17
Liverpool - 188
Lloyd George - 57, 84, 85
lobbying - 29
local county elections - 7
Local Education Authorities - 14, 181
London - 22
Lord Beaverbrook - 57
Lord Chancellor - 12, 47, 96
Lord Chief Justice - 84
Lord Clinton-Davis - 67
Lord Grigson - 67
Lord Hambro - 73
Lord Haskel - 67
Lord Healey - 70
Lord Home - 134
Lord Irvine - 12
Lord Mackay - 95
Lord Marshall of Knightsbridge - 63
Lord Neill's - 56, 77
Lord Nolan - 55, 77

INDEX

Lord Nolan's inquiry - 55
Lord Sainsbury - 69
Lord Salisbury - 83
Lord Shaftesbury - 83
Lord Simon of Highbury - 63
Lord Wyatt of Weeford - 61
Lord Younger - 74
lottery schemes - 21, 200
Louise Recivieur - 158
Luftwaffe - 115
Luxembourg - 134
Maastricht - 139
Maastricht European Treaty - 98, 139, 147, 148
MAFF - 59
Magna Carta - 106
Mail on Sunday - 49
Malaysian Pergau Dam - 202
Manchester - 82, 111, 188
manifesto - 30
Marconi Company - 84
Margaret Thatcher - 58, 88, 98, 113, 137
Marlowe - 108
Marta Andreasen - 161
Mary - 107
Mary of Holland - 109
Max Aitken - 57
Mayonic Public Relations - 158
Mayor Giuliani - 187, 188
McCawley - 89
Members of Parliament - 9, 50
MEPs - 159, 162
Michael Ashcroft - 75
Michael Griffith - 61
Michael O'Leary - 152
Michael Trend - 49
Middle East - 86
mileage allowance - 47
military forces - 102
mining - 83
Minister Bidault - 131
Minister for Trade and Competitiveness - 63
Minister for War - 87
Ministry of Agriculture - 59

Ministry of Defence - 73, 75
Mohamad Hashemi - 72
monarch - 32
monkey - 7
Monnet - 131, 133, 137
Morecombe Bay - 190
Mori - 33
Mr Connolly - 139
Mr Fasting - 157
Mr François - 156
Mr Ojo - 162
Mr. Blunkett - 189
Mrs Edith Cresson - 158
Mrs Wallis Warfield Simpson - 113
Munich - 114
Nadir - 72
Nancy Astor - 88
Napoleon - 130
Napoleonic wars - 111
National Audit Office - 154
National Curriculum Council - 181
National Executive - 71
National Institute for Clinical Excellence - 176
national parks - 6
National Rivers Authority - 59
National Security - 26
National Trust - 66
National Westminster Bank - 71
NATO - 95, 146
Nazis - 114, 115
Nazi-Soviet pact - 85, 114
Nazmu Virani - 72
NDPBs - 60
Neil Kinnock - 161
Nellie Maes - 159
Nelson - 111
Nesta organisation - 198
Netherlands (the) - 118, 134
New Labour - 32, 44, 45, 50, 66, 67, 68, 71
New York - 186, 187
New Zealand - 6, 15, 16
NGO - 60
NHS - 61, 88, 175, 179, 193

Nicholas Jones - 44
Nissan UK - 153
No '10' Downing Street - 44
nolle prosequi - 98
Normans (the) - 105
Norman Lamont - 140
Normandy - 105
Northern Cyprus - 72
Northern Ireland - 104
Northern Ireland Executive - 150
Norway - 6, 77, 105, 114, 115, 145, 149, 204
OBE - 57
Octav Botnar - 72
OFSTED - 181, 183
Ohio - 86
OLAF - 162
Old Sarum - 112
Oliver Cromwell - (see Cromwell)
'On the Record' television programme - 68
Opposition parties - 43
Order of the British Empire - 57
Orkney - 104
Oxfam - 202
Oxford - 80
Palace of Westminster - 75
Panorama - 160
Parliament - 19, 45, 46, 48, 94
Parliamentary Codes and Ethics - 77
Parliamentary Commissioner for Standards -
46, 50, 56
Parliamentary initiatives - 18
Parliament Reform Catechism- 82
Patrick Dixon - 49
patronage - 43, 60
Paul Drayson - 67
Paul Gann - 30
Paul van Buitenen - 145, 154
Paul-Henri Spaak - 130, 131
payroll vote - 53
peers - 51, 97
Pension audit trails - 195
People's Chancellor - 25, 28, 206
Peregrine Worsthorne - 198

Peter Mandelson - 7, 69
Peterloo Massacre - 111
petition - 15, 20
Petition of Rights - 80
Philip Norton - 97
Police Standards Unit - 185
politicians' salaries - 6, 12
polling stations - 21
Polly Peck - 71, 72
Popular initiative - 17
Popular veto - 19
Powderject Pharmaceuticals - 67
Premier Club - 75
Presbyterian faith - 110
President - 9
President Charles de Gaulle - 134, 135
President George Bush - 119
President J. F. Kennedy - 86
President Pompidou - 135
Price of Power - 71
Pricewaterhouse Coopers - 66
Primary Care Trust - 175
Prime Minister Bhutto - 56
Prince Regent - 82
prison sentencing - 99
private day-schools - 180
Privy Council - 106, 118
privy councillors - 44
Professor Peter Schroeder - 64
Profumo - 87
property qualifications - 111
proposal - 18
Protestants - 107, 109
Public Appointments Unit - 61
Public Policy Unit - 55
Qualifications and Curriculum Authority - 181
quangos - 44, 53, 58, 59
Queen Anne - 110
Queen Elizabeth II (see Elizabeth II)
Queen Victoria - 112
Queen's Speech - 50
Radovan Karadzic - 73
railways - 83

referendum - 15, 17, 19, 20, 24, 25, 27, 28, 30

Reform Act - 111, 112

Register of Members' Interests - 48, 67

Renault - 153

'representative' democracy - 9, 10, 103

Republicanism - 119

resettlement grant - 48

River Thames - 80, 84

Robert Fleming Bankers - 74

Romania - 68

Romans - 104

Rome - 107

Royal Air Force - 115

Royal Bank of Scotland - 74

Royal Charter - 118

Royal College of Veterinary Surgeons - 118

Royal Consent - 110

Royal Navys - 114

Royal Prerogative - 97

Rudy Giuliani - 186

Ruhr Valley - 131

Runnymede - 106

Russia - 86, 133

Russian Mafia - 160

Ryan Air - 152

SAS - 150

Save the Children - 202

Saxons - 105

Scapa Flow - 114

Scarborough - 179

Scotland - 16, 81, 104, 108, 110

Scottish Affairs Select Committee - 45

Scottish Parliament - 110

second chamber - 32

Second World War - 130, 135

secret ballots - 111

secret lobbying - 43

Secretary of State - 45, 61, 64

Secretary-General Trojan - 159

Select Committee - 45, 46, 54

Select Committees - 45

Senate - 9

Serious Fraud Squad - 72

Sevenoaks - 17

Shakespeare - 108

shareholders - 196

Shetlands - 104

shipping - 83

Shoreham - 17

Short Money - 76

Simon Jenkins - 102

Single European Act - 63, 138

Single Regeneration Budget - 144

Sir Francis Drakes - 108

Sir Isaac Newton - 109

Sir John Drughorn - 57

Sir Joseph Robinson - 57

Sir Philip Mawer - 50

Sir William Vestey - 57

sleaze - 43

socialist societies - 70

Somerset - 105

South Atlantic - 98

sovereignty of Parliament - 96

Soviet Bloc - 61

Spain - 16, 107, 109, 111, 117

Spanish Armada - 108

special contingency allowance - 48

Spin - 43

St Osyth - 17

staffing allowance - 47

Stamford Bridge - 105

Standards and Privileges Committee - 50

Standing Committees - 54

Steve John - 54

Steve Moxon - 190

Strasbourg - 138

Stuart Weir - 62

Sudeten Lands - 85

Suez - 86, 116

supplementary allowance - 47

Sussex - 105

Sweden - 6, 77

Swinging Sixties - 87

Switzerland - 6, 11, 15, 16, 27, 28, 32, 72, 145, 149, 204, 207, 210, 215

Taiwan - 87
TAO - 155
Task Force Groups - 60
tax evasion - 57
taxation - 6
Teacher Training Agency - 181
Technical Assistance Offices - 155
temporary staff allowance - 47
Teresa Gorman - 52
Thomas Paine - 111
Tony Benn - 55
Tony Blair - 44, 67, 68, 69, 98, 99, 141
Tony Blair's special advisors - 120
Tories (see Conservatives) - 85, 89, 112
Touche Ross - 72
Tourist Board - 61
Tower of London - 81
trade unions - 70, 87, 89, 136
Treaties of Rome and Paris - 134
Treaty of Rome - 133
Treaty of the European Union - 139
UK Polar Medal Assessment Committee - 59
Unionists - 76
United Nations - 86, 95, 189
United Nations Convention on Refugees - 189
United States of America - 7, 9, 16, 25, 31, 33,
56, 85, 86, 87, 130, 132, 133, 134, 146, 187
'Urban' initiative - 144
VAT - 13, 29, 143, 148
Viceroy of India - 84
Vlaamse Volksunie - 159
Voyage of Discovery - 108
W.M. Mercer - 12
Wakefield Crown Court - 88
Wales - 16, 81, 83, 104
'weapons of mass destruction' - 45
Wessex - 105
West Midlands regional health authority - 59
Westminster - 7, 26, 43, 45, 80, 86, 109
Whigs (also see Liberals) - 83
Whips - 43, 46, 52
Whitehall - 81
Wick's committee - 46

William of Normandy - 105, 109
William Haig - 75
William IV - 111
William of Normandy - 104, 105
Wilson (Harold) - 87, 137
Wiltshire - 17, 105
winding-up allowance - 48
Winston Churchill - 85, 114, 116, 131
Winter of Discontent - 87
women voting - 26
World Bank - 95
World Trade Organisation - 95
written constitution - 18, 26, 100
www.directdemocracyinternational.com - 205
Wyre Forest - 179
Yugoslavia - 73, 147
Zelijko Raznatovic - 73